HOPE IS NOT A STRATEGY

Leadership Lessons from the Obama Presidency

D. M. LUKAS
JOHN L. MARIOTTI

Award Winning Author of *The Complexity Crisis*

HOPE IS NOT A STRATEGY: Leadership Lessons from the Obama Presidency

ISBN: 1469931044
ISBN 13: 9781469931043

DISCLAIMER

This book provides general information that is intended to inform and educate the reader on a general basis. Every effort has been made to assure that the information contained herein is accurate and timely as of the date of publication. However, it is provided for the convenience of the reader only. THE AUTHOR, PUBLISHER AND ALL AFFILIATED PARTIES EXPRESSLY DISCLAIM ANY AND ALL EXPRESS OR IMPLIED WARRANTIES, INCLUDING THE IMPLIED WARRANTY OF MERCHANTABILITY AND FITNESS FOR A PARTICULAR PURPOSE. The information presented herein may not be suitable for each reader's particular situation. It is recommended that each reader consult a professional in the reader's respective discipline for further advice on this subject. Reliance on information in this book is at the reader's sole risk. In no event are the Authors, Publisher or any affiliated party liable for any direct, indirect, incidental, consequential, or other damages of any kind whatsoever including lost profits, relative to the information or advice provided herein. Reference to any specific commercial product, process or service, does not constitute and endorsements or recommendation. The authors have taken all possible precautions to verify information in the book, but since certain parts of it were obtained from public information and news reports, which might have been in error, verifying the accuracy was not possible in some cases. Sources of secondary material are footnoted when the sources were known and/or identified.

INTRODUCTION: HOPE IS NOT A STRATEGY

Authors' Note

The phrase "Hope is not a strategy" was first used in recent times by Benjamin Ola Akande, an economist, scholar, and Dean of the Business School at Webster University in Saint Louis in an open letter to President Barack Obama in 2009. What Akande meant was that Obama – and any other president – needed to act. He cannot wish away problems. There must be a concentrated effort to solve problems and to increase opportunities. Sitting around thinking about how the current situation could be better would not change anything. Certainly, hope and prayer can help, but one must also be prepared to do his/her part in achieving the goal.

Our purpose in this book is less to be critical of Barack Obama and his presidency, and more to find the lessons in the mistakes made, so they are less likely to be repeated. We believe that failures represent some of life's greatest learning opportunities. By taking these very public and very painful failures and extracting the lessons from them, we hope to help generations to come to avoid those mistakes—and those failures.

Most of all, we believe these lessons can be transferred to the world of business—especially in the United States of America. It is our fervent goal that many of these lessons will help Americans in all walks of life be more successful, and they, in turn, will help our great nation return to economic growth and prosperity.

D. M. Lukas
John Mariotti

I
LEADERSHIP

"Your actions speak so loudly, I cannot hear your words."

—Stephen R. Covey

CHAPTER ONE

STYLE IS MORE IMPORTANT THAN SUBSTANCE—TEMPORARILY

A presidency starts out first and foremost as a "sales" job. When the job is President of the United States of America, it could be the biggest and most important—and challenging—sales position in the world. The president must be able to constantly and consistently "make the sale" to a hugely diverse group of constituencies.

Great salespeople often have great style and for many great salespeople, style is all they ever need because they have great teams behind them to back them up and deliver on their promises. Unfortunately, the presidency doesn't work that way. The Presidency quickly becomes a leadership job, and an enormously complex management challenge. Those sales skills are still necessary—to "sell" the positions and decisions—but the results rely on substance.

It not only takes great style, but solid substance to back up the many decisions a President must make and then implement. Style can definitely help win the position, as we have seen. Barack Obama's "style" was certainly a huge factor in helping him defeat

John McCain. Once in office, as Obama found (and so many others have learned) to be effective you must have the substance to go with the style.

If you are in a position of leadership and realize that you have great style, but may be lacking in the substance to keep you there, take some time to seek out those who have the substance you need, to help you learn what you need to learn, to perform in your position, and grow further in your own substance.

In his best selling books, Stephen Covey[1] differentiates a "personality-based leader" (looking good) from a "principle-based leader" (doing good). Style—"looking good" vs. "doing good," — is a very superficial way for a leader to operate. The likelihood of being exposed when relying too greatly on style is high, because the outcomes tell the story of success or failure. Style may get you noticed, and even "liked," but the downside of that is closer scrutiny, which will quickly reveal any lack of substance behind the style.

In experience, we have all seen many instances of the "up and comer," who gets promoted several times based on style, but with a modest amount of substantive achievement. However, at some level the "Peter Principle"[2] kicks in and the "up and comer" plateaus.

The problems of the Obama presidency and the lessons from it will be revealed repeatedly to contain two major "lacks:" lack of leadership and management experience and the lack of the right policy direction. Experience, or the lack thereof, is where the substance required becomes more tangible, more evident and more critical. The absence of substance, and over-reliance on style, quickly shows in stressful situations. Substance stands the tests of

---

1 Covey, Stephen R. *Seven Habits of Highly Effective Leaders* Fireside: Simon & Schuster. New York, NY. 1989, and *Principle-Centered Leadership* Fireside: Simon & Schuster. New York, NY. 1990 & 1991

2 The **"Peter Principle"** says "in a hierarchy every employee tends to rise to his level of incompetence", meaning that people tend to get promoted upward until they reach a position at which they are no longer competent. This was described by Dr. Laurence J. Peter and Raymond Hull in their humorous book *The Peter Principle* Morrow. 1969.

pressure and scrutiny. It is consistent, and has an authority to it that no stylish presentation alone can deliver. Policy deficiencies just complicate this lack of substance further

Remember, as Barack Obama has found, "you don't know what you don't know—and some of what you think you know, isn't so." But in Barack Obama's case he thinks he knows everything. He seems to think he is the smartest person in the room, no matter who else is there.

You must seek out experienced staff and mentors to help you to learn what "you don't know." It is only through this combination of experience and knowledge that the temporary benefit of "style" can be supported with the enduring attribute of "substance."

OBAMA PRESIDENCY BACKGROUND AND TYPICAL ISSUES

Barack Obama rose from political obscurity to the national limelight by virtue of his rousing speech at the 2004 Democratic National Convention, in which he appealed to the country to once again become the "United" States of America. During his campaign, he made speech after teleprompter-aided speech, building on this "style."

Obama became really good at this. People loved him and his campaign theme "Hope & Change." Therein were born his error and our lesson. A speech, no matter how great, is only a tool. There must be substance supporting it. Style is only a valid longer-term asset if there is something meaningful behind it. Martin Luther King's "I Have A Dream" speech was underpinned by a life of substance and solid experience. Ronald Reagan's, "Mr. Gorbachev, tear down this wall…" line was based on his prior actions and accomplishments.

Obama's "style," at which he became so adept, was only supported by the thinnest of resumes and the superficial substance of an aspiring candidate. As Obama climbed to the nomination and then won the presidency, the grandeur of his speeches and the magnitude of his style grew to immense proportions. Enormous, enthusiastic crowds elevated Obama to "rock star" stature—in style. But here was a man who had led little or nothing of any size or consequence, and whose experience in governing was very limited.

Thus the first lesson is that style can seem more important than substance, but only temporarily. Then the lack of substance in some reasonable proportion to the style becomes a glaring shortcoming.

∾

"You can't talk your way out of what you've behaved yourself into."

—Stephen R. Covey

∾

CHAPTER TWO

SPEECHES ARE NOT PLANS— OR STRATEGIES

You can dazzle a group with a great speech. You can give a "rah-rah" speech that gets everyone excited, but most of the time the effect only lasts for a short time. The reaction "When in doubt, make a speech" leads to the question, "then what?" The speech is only the start; there must be a plan or a strategy behind the speech or the words ring false or hollow. Speeches can inform, inspire and enthuse an audience but without a call to action, and a strategy to follow, the energy created quickly dissipates. What is more important than just giving a speech and painting a vision, is having a plan that is understandable and that your audience can feel a share in making it happen.

There have been some wonderful "speeches" throughout history, but the ones you remember most were the ones by people that not only gave them, but also went out and made their words into a reality. Well-delivered speeches are wonderful tools to engage, inform, inspire and motivate an audience, but when there is no strategy behind them, no evidence of a plan to deliver on the promises, and few calls to action, the speech is a hollow vessel.

Don't make these hollow speeches; make speeches that are backed by substantive plans and executable strategies.

Leaders like Winston Churchill, Abraham Lincoln, Martin Luther King, (and even Jesus Christ!) are known so well and studied, because they actually helped make what they described become a reality. The speakers not only declared it, but also they had a plan and strategy, which showed others how to make it happen—and how to continue once they were long gone.

Before you deliver a message, whether it is to a large audience or just a few people, think through the strategy of how to make what you talking about a reality, and how you will get people excited about doing that. Make sure you lay out a clear and concise path to the outcome you desire. When you make promises to people, either in fact, or by innuendo, you create expectations: that you will actually follow through, and do what you spoke of doing. If those expectations are not met, if there is no follow through, and no action, the people will become less motivated than they were initially.

Another problem occurs when speeches lay out "grand plans," which have no underpinning. Today's "always-on" media captures spoken words with frightening thoroughness. A leader can no longer claim, "I never said that." At most their lament might be "I never meant that," or "I misspoke." Any of these claims invalidates the power of the speech, if and when parts of the audience compare words and action.

In politics, opponents are quick to point out flaws, misstatements and broken promises. In business, the audiences are stakeholders of many kinds. They too notice disconnects between glowing words and/or promises and lackluster results. And they become concerned, demotivated, and sometimes, downright angry, feeling betrayed and misled.

If strategies and actions back up the words in a speech, there is "meat on the bones" of the statements made. If not, the words of the speech may sound fine; they may even evoke the desired emotions in listeners, but sooner or later those who heard the words would find them hollow and neither credible nor convincing.

All stakeholders: voters, business owners, customers, employees, suppliers, communities and many others can evaluate the statements by looking for the underlying strategies, and decide on the soundness and reasonableness of the words compared to the likely actions. This point is the very core of credibility for any leader, including a manager or a politician—or for anyone else who makes a speech. A wise man once said, "Say what you plan to do—then do what you said—or don't say it in the first place."

OBAMA PRESIDENCY BACKGROUND AND TYPICAL ISSUES

Over and over again President Obama has cited grand hopes and lofty ambitions in his speeches, but failed to follow them with the actual strategies and executional details to make them into realities. None were more obviously discounted than his speech during the budget spending limit debates in which he claimed to have "laid out a plan." To this the head of the General Accounting Office, when asked to evaluate the economics of Obama's "plan," said, "We can't value a speech—we need details."

ᕲ

"Giving money and power to government is like giving whiskey and car keys to teenage boys."

—P.J. O'Rourke

ᕲ

CHAPTER THREE

Don't Change Your Values to Fit Your Audiences

Saying whatever an audience wants to hear is perilous—because what they want to hear changes constantly, and that may not be what's best to do. There are so many different pairs of ears in an audience that many of them will hear different parts of what is said, according to what they believe and want to hear. That is simply how people operate: they listen selectively.

This is where President Obama not only created great momentum but also has gotten himself in the most trouble, by telling audiences what he believed they wanted to hear. His values and message seem to change constantly to fit the audience he is with at that particular moment. As such, he has made it very hard to trust what he says from day to day, as he often contradicts himself.

Presidential candidates, including GOP hopeful Mitt Romney, have also been accused of this characteristic. Notable differences are (in Romney's case) when the so-called "flip flops" involve moves from policies that served the constituents of a particular state, to policies for serving a national constituency, or results from studies providing new information, led to different positions. The other notable difference is that in Obama's case, the contrast is between what he said he would do as a candidate and what he has actually done as a sitting president. That is a very big, different and significant kind of "flip flop."

Obama also creates a dilemma for himself when addressing a very large, mixed audience (such as a national speech). In this situation, he often moves back and forth ("flip-flops"), within the same speech, trying to please various segments of the audience, but leaving many of them confused about what his real positions are. The only times he effectively stays "on topic" is when he is attacking an opponent, which is why he likes "campaign style" speeches so much, or "selling" one of his pet projects.

"Saying what they want to hear" works well for people that won't take responsibility or accountability for those statements. But for people that must be accountable (especially leaders), "saying what they want to hear" or changing your values in doing so, is a surefire way to lose respect, credibility, and ultimately the ability to lead. Stakeholders, especially employees and investors, detect such devious behavior very quickly.

What is important is to tell audiences "what is important" and to repeat it consistently over and over. Constancy of purpose is one of the most notable and memorable aspects of a leader. In many cases, members of the audience only hear the message that one time, although the leader may have said it many times. Hearing the same message over and over—with the same content—even if the words vary, helps reinforce the truthfulness and consistency that people value so much.

However, when the message is "modified" to fit the wishes of different audiences, the larger aggregate audience does not hear the same message. They hear many different versions of it. This may satisfy the less thoughtful, shallower thinkers, but it will concern any who consider what was really being said and make comparisons over time. The always on, 24/7/365 media does this relentlessly—when it suits their purposes.

In Barack Obama's case, he would even change his speech patterns to fit the audience, or say things that play to the perceived beliefs of his audience. Remember the "clinging to their guns and religion" comment to a group of wealthy, aristocratic liberals? If he truly believed in that statement, why was it he never said it in the heartland of America, where it was aimed?

During his presidential campaign, candidate Obama spoke like a "moderate," and his plans, promises and platform were designed to attract the largest possible range of voters. His strongest supporters knew (or believed) that he was still a dedicated liberal at heart—and they would support any Democratic candidate anyway. Thus, Obama, like many candidates, attracted voters by intentionally but skillfully misleading them.

In business, doing this is a sure-fire way to create turnover of your best employees. Many of the best and brightest in companies "buy into" the philosophy, the culture and the mission/vision of the business. They also "buy into" the character of their leaders. Mislead them, lie to them, or change positions constantly, the best people will realize that they probably don't belong there—and leave.

In politics, since voting is a one-time event, candidates get away with misleading positions or "pandering" to audiences—once, anyway. In business, where the statements and behavior are ongoing, and observed on more of a day-to-day basis, any such manipulation usually becomes more noticeable.

As a leader, or simply as a person of integrity, you must know yourself, your values and who you are, and never compromise your values to "get ahead," or influence an audience. You will find that even if you succeed, that success is short-lived. Once exposed, you will quickly come crashing back down, losing the ability to get back on top...perhaps permanently.

OBAMA PRESIDENCY BACKGROUND AND TYPICAL ISSUES

Barack Obama campaigned as a "moderate" telling most of his audiences what they wanted to hear—and weaving back and forth—never quite revealing how liberal his policies would be once converted into legislation. Thus he disappointed both supporters in the moderate group by being too liberal, and his "base" of liberal supporters, by being too moderate. Pandering to an audience by altering your apparent values is a very dangerous game indeed.

༄

"In general, the art of government consists of taking as much money as possible from one party of the citizens to give to the other."

—Voltaire (1764)

༄

CHAPTER FOUR

YOU NEVER WIN PITTING GROUPS IN AN ORGANIZATION AGAINST EACH OTHER

Is "the enemy of my enemy, my friend?" Not for long! Creating internal conflict is a self-defeating behavior. The most effective organizations have unity—of purpose, of culture and of goals and strategies for attaining those goals. Pitting people within any group or organization against each other may seem to create healthy competition, but it is usually divisive and damaging to the organization overall. Soon everyone wonders what agenda the other people are trying to pursue—rather than all pulling together toward common goals and a shared vision.

Obama is often accused of "class warfare," pitting one group or class against another in attempt to achieve political gain. In President Obama's case it is not so much for political gain per se, but to cover for his lack of leadership. "If you are not happy with the economy...blame the rich," has been one of his favorite mantras. In reality, the reason that the economy is struggling is not "the rich," but the fact that there is very little certainty—and less optimism—in the private sector during his tenure. Thus the private sector shuns many growth opportunities.

The reason very little certainty exists is because Obama, as discussed in Chapter 2, has not articulated a viable plan or a clear strategy for success—and the initiatives he has undertaken have failed to produce the promised results. Clarity about the prevailing environment (especially regarding likely government actions) is a must for businesses and individuals to make longer-term decisions. Absent that, they "sit on the sidelines" and wait, while the economy struggles, paralyzed by uncertainty. Adding to that, fear about "anti-business" policies heightens the tendency of businesses not to invest in growth.

The blame of gridlock due to partisan divisiveness is another worrisome factor. Obama ran as a "uniter" but has governed as a "divider." Part of the divisiveness is purposely built into the governmental constitutional structure of the United States. It was done to create a series of checks and balances, to keep any one faction from becoming too powerful, acting too quickly and/or disenfranchising any large groups of Americans. Thus Congress must advise and consent on Presidential appointments; the Congress initiates legislation, which must pass votes through both the House and the Senate and then be signed into law by the president. Most recently, President Obama's actions have thwarted even these Constitutional safeguards.[3]

This difficult and circuitous process makes governing hard; bi-partisanship is much more a word than a reality in today's polarized political climate. This leaves American government in a semi-permanent state of gridlock and paralysis. The Founding Fathers planned on "leadership" by the president to help work through such impasses. Not only has Barack Obama not fulfilled that leadership role. He has added fuel to the dis-unity as he fails

---

3 The recess appointments of Richard Cordray and several members of the NLRB were in direct violation of the Constitutional ban on "recess appointments" when the Senate is not actually in recess. Proof that it was not in recess is evidenced by the fact that it approved the president's two-month extension of the payroll tax reduction, and yet, the President went ahead with the appointments anyway.

to lead the opposing groups to necessary outcomes—even small compromises to make progress.

Obama's most important speech, at the Democratic National Convention in 2004, was marked by this statement: "…Now even as we speak, there are those who are preparing to divide us, the spin masters, the negative ad peddlers who embrace the politics of anything goes. Well, I say to them tonight, there is not a liberal America and a conservative America — there is the United States of America. …" How many readers believe that his actions as President have matched these inspiring words? Not very many!

In your position of leadership, you must not divide people, but find ways to bring them together to accomplish a common goal or task. You must have clarity in your purpose, your plan, and your actions. You must communicate clearly and directly—and admit that some people might not like the planned direction as much as others, but that you want them to come along too. Consensus is not always unanimous; sometimes compromise is necessary to make progress. Collaboration is not always single-minded, and compromise is not always enjoyable—but it is necessary. All of these—clarity… in communication, collaboration… to reach consensus and/or compromise—are critical to success in business, in politics—and in life. Otherwise, you will find that you too will "drift along" without any meaningful results or perfect solutions— and you will lose respect for your leadership, especially when it doesn't help bring about unity.

Dale Carnegie said it best in his book, <u>How to Win Friends and Influence People</u>,[4] "Never criticize, condemn, or complain about someone or a group." You will find a lot more success by finding ways to bring people together from different sides rather than dividing them. America's Founding Fathers "coined" the words: E pluribus unum. (Out of many, one.) Which still appear to this day on our money—as a reminder to us about national unity. The phrase "United we stand, divided we fall," used by Patrick Henry in his famous 1799 speech, is as true today—over two hundred

---

4 Dale Carnegie. *How to Win and Influence People*, Simon & Schuster. New York, NY. 1936

years later—as it was then. Uniters win; dividers lose; it's as simple as that.

OBAMA PRESIDENCY BACKGROUND AND TYPICAL ISSUES

Many of President Obama's opponents accuse him of "class warfare." Whether this term applies precisely is beside the point. His actions as president have been so far from his 2004 appeal to "unite" the country that few would argue in his favor. Obama's claims to desire bi-partisan government quickly evaporated in the face of continued rejection of his liberal-leaning policies. Thus, all he could do is try to pit members of Congress against each other, and hope to win in that process. No one wins in internecine warfare; the only question is who loses bigger. The answer is usually the initiator. To this, we ask what has become of the man who told us in 2004: "Well, I say to them tonight, there is not a liberal America and a conservative America — there is the United States of America."

∾

"If you don't read the newspaper you are uninformed; if you do read the newspaper you are misinformed."

—Mark Twain

∾

CHAPTER FIVE

INTEGRITY IS YOUR MOST IMPORTANT ASSET

This may be the most important chapter in this book. As far as we are concerned, integrity is the one thing that you must never compromise. It is the one thing that, above all else, will help you to lead up to your true potential. Lastly, your integrity and reputation will define you as a person to those around you.

Don't devalue integrity or give it up; walk your talk—or else. You can't fool "the troops." Integrity is like virginity—either you have it or you don't. There is no "half-way." Integrity is also relies upon trust.

Building trust is a lot like inflating a balloon. It takes a lot of time and effort to blow it up, but let it go for just one short moment, and all of the effort is wasted. Trust takes time to build, but can be lost in an instant. It is extremely hard to regain trust with people once you have lost it.

The only proof of integrity is behavior—words and actions— and those do not lie. President Barack Obama, over the course of his first term, has shown his lack of integrity, especially with

many of the people that put him office—the independent voters of the American electorate. When Obama was elected, it was
widely noted that the independent vote is what helped him to win.
Through his first term, he has steadily lost support from the independent voters, to the point that it is now less than half of what it
was when he was elected.

What is the primary reason for this loss? A failure of integrity.
Obama has consistently changed his leadership style, positions and
direction away from what he campaigned on. This ranges from
practicing class warfare, and running as a "uniter," to promising
transparency and then passing bills before they are even looked
at (Obamacare), to even flat-out lying (he stated he would have
no lobbyists on his staff and to date there are over 40—and that is
only one of many instances of lies and broken promises).

"But all politicians lie," is what people often say. This is a feeble
and sorry excuse. It may explain why Americans hold politicians
in such low regard. When the approval ratings for our Congress
hover consistently below 20%, something is clearly wrong. When
only one-third of Americans think the country is headed in the
right direction under President Obama, trust in his leadership
has clearly been lost. In the chapters that follow, we will describe
many lessons to be learned from Obama's leadership failures that
have led to this sorry situation.

Some would blame this public lack of confidence on the
difficulty of the situations faced by our leaders. That is not a
valid or sufficient excuse. There are always difficult situations,
and it is in those times that the strength and integrity of the
leaders must shine through. The old saw, "When the going
gets tough, the tough get going," is not just an idle play on
words. It is true. Besides, these people, our leaders, weren't
forced into the positions; they actively campaigned and asked
for them!

Considering many years of experience, there are some timeless
truths that remain immutable and unchanged. A leader must have
more than integrity; s/he must also have competence, courage and
character. These three attributes may not be sufficient, but they are

certainly necessary. The competence is about knowing what to do and/or how to do it; the courage is about doing it, when it is incredibly difficult; and the character is all about having the integrity to be true to the values and principles, which are the guide posts everyone needs to stay the course in difficult times. These truths are true in business and in government. Violating them compromises your most important asset as a leader—your reputation.

That most important asset—reputation—is one that we all have, and it is based on integrity. The respect that you receive from being trusted, trustworthy and truthful with all that you do to lead and interact with people is almost impossible to replace once lost. Certainly there will be situations where there is no "good" solution, just a series of "bad" ones. It is in these times that integrity serves you most and best. As a leader, you must put your integrity ahead of your ambitions and strive to do the right thing in every situation. Doing the right thing is often easier than knowing the right thing to do, but both are imperatives for leadership.

OBAMA PRESIDENCY BACKGROUND AND TYPICAL ISSUES

Few things impugn integrity more or faster than being caught in an outright lie. When a person gives as many speeches that are recorded and televised as candidate Obama and President Obama, it is almost impossible to not get caught in lies. Many argue that all politicians lie; but this is not an excuse for repeatedly misstating, distorting or outright lying about facts in order to twist the truth into an ally when it is an unwilling one. A simple YouTube video chronicles just one of many such examples: http://www.city-data.com/forum/politics-other-controversies/795444-7-lies-under-2-minutes.html

୧୨

"The ultimate result of shielding men from the effects of folly is to fill the world with fools."

—Herbert Spencer, (English Philosopher 1820-1903)

CHAPTER SIX

WHAT DO YOU DO WHEN NOBODY IS FOLLOWING YOUR LEAD?

Look in the mirror. Ask yourself if anyone is following you, or are you "being run out of town?" If no one is following you, then you are not a leader. You may be in a leadership position, but that does not necessarily mean that you are a "leader."

People look to leaders to take them to places they would be afraid to go alone. They also want leaders that will go along, and in doing so, prove their commitment to the journey. If you want people to follow you, you have to be willing to "get down in the trenches" with them and help them succeed (not spend your time on the golf course or take extended vacations and countless fund-raising trips while they struggle with tough times.)

True leaders understand that it is not the position that makes them a leader, but the ability to show people a vision of the future, to help them get there, and to expose and utilize talents and capabilities that the people never even knew they had. In short, you must bring out the best in those around you, and not be afraid to work alongside of them to show your belief in them.

Leaders exude their leadership. This cannot be described in words, but people can sense it—or not. They will follow true leaders, and not trust, nor follow the pretenders. Barack Obama has shown an incredible lack of accomplishment in this area. Many have labeled him as a narcissist and that may be part of the problem.

His real problem is that people can see how much he is faking that he cares. He strains to show empathy and is always looking for the right sound bite, but his expressions and body language betray him. His reliance on Teleprompters for almost every speech showed that he dared not get off script, because if he did people could not relate to him, or even identify with his message. Or worse, they might learn what his real thoughts and policies were ("I just want to spread the wealth around, etc.")—or that they were so vague that he really had none.

Genuine leaders are usually "servant leaders" and they are more concerned with leading their followers to the right places, in the right ways, and proving that constancy of purpose in every-thing they say and do, and in every decision they make.

Barack Obama's presidency always seems so much more con-cerned with "what the polls will say" or "what will get him ree-lected" than what really needs to be done. As Obama has strayed from his campaign rhetoric, he has also become increasingly lib-eral (some say socialistic) in his words, in his decisions, and in his policies. His actions have increasingly been in conflict with his words. This is a sure sign of a leadership failure.

This president is attempting to lead a country that was founded on freedom and the ability for any individual to achieve as much as they can—but he is doing it in a way that is contrary to those ide-als. Increasingly, Obama's "government-knows-best" philosophy has driven more people away from him than it has drawn to follow him. In short, he is making a serious leadership mistake, doing almost the exact opposite of what he led many of his constituents to expect. He is not helping them to reach their potential, and seems less and less interested in doing so as each day passes.

Campaigning for reelection is now preeminent with President Obama. Any and all decisions and statements are weighed against this goal. Avoiding any more blemishes on his record also seems to be his primary goal—even to the exclusion of his responsibility to govern and/or do what is right for America. His words make good sound bites, but have no substance or potential for success, except as campaign ploys. Thus fewer and fewer people want to follow his leadership. Obama's frustration with the job of governing is also palpable and evident.

This brings up another important lesson to keep in mind. People believe in and follow leaders who do not show their frustration, but do show determination and a positive, can-do attitude. True leaders do not whine; they do not blame others for their failures; and they do not make excuses. Barack Obama does all three—and frequently.

As a leader, you must always be conscious of the fact that it is not the leader that makes results happen. It is those around the leader, following the leader proactively, and giving themselves to the goal because they believe in the leader and their purpose. That is what makes the leader ultimately successful. There is a difference between being a leader and being a manager (or steward) and the former is one of the differences.

A metaphor helps explain the difference between a leader and a manager. If there is a group trip to be taken, the manager makes sure the route is well mapped and the provisions and supplies are adequate. The leader inspires the group to want to make the trip—and for the right reasons.

The current occupant of the White House also lacks the respect of Congress—even including some members of his own party. Barack Obama's inexperience and his obvious unwillingness to do the hard, day-to-day work of governing are evident to them. He always thinks his ideas are better than theirs, and it shows. When they don't do what he wants, he becomes impatient, petulant and scolds them. Then he tours the country and criticizes them from afar. Thus he cannot lead the government of the United States effectively, because too few are willing to follow him! This is also why he also seems ineffective when he is among foreign leaders. They sense his leadership deficiencies, in spite of his eloquent rhetoric, and in the process, lose respect for America as well.

Barack Obama has neither spent the time, nor devoted the effort to earn his leadership position, except by his superb campaign skills (mostly making speeches)—and that is not enough. Remember, style runs out quickly when there is no substance underpinning it.

OBAMA PRESIDENCY BACKGROUND AND TYPICAL ISSUES

The debt-ceiling impasse of mid-2011 was a classic case of President Obama trying to lead when no one was following. The President finally stalked out of meetings in fits of frustration and/or pique, allowing the leaders of both parties to choose their own approaches and collaborate on a proposed resolution to the debt ceiling issue. Few failures are more devastating to a leader that being unable to gain the support and involvement of critical "followers." Obama's external manifestation was then to make an angry speech, in which he scolded Congress about "staying there at work" in Washington to resolve matters—at which point he left for a series of campaign fund raisers, followed by an extended vacation on Martha's Vineyard. It is no surprise that his governmental counterparts are not enthused about following his leadership

༄

"Leaders take people to places they would be afraid to go alone— and go along."

—Robert Galvin, Sr., (Former Chairman & CEO of Motorola)

༄

II
EXPERIENCE AND PEOPLE

"In theory, there is no difference between theory and practice; in practice there is a hell of a lot of difference."

CHAPTER SEVEN

There's No Substitute for Real Experience

When thinking of this chapter title, an old Rodney Dangerfield movie, "Back to School" comes to mind. In the movie, Dangerfield portrays a successful businessman who never attended college. To help his discouraged son get through college, he makes the decision to go to school with him.

There is a scene where Rodney is in an economics class with a particularly snide professor, who does not seem to like him, and they are discussing setting up a business.

The professor starts out by talking about setting up a factory to which Rodney asks, "What is the product?" The professor sneers at him and says that it doesn't matter, but "for this case, let's just say it is tape recorders."

Rodney laughs and replies, "Are you kidding? The Japanese will kill us on labor costs!"

The professor says, "Ok then, lets just call them widgets."

Rodney replies, "What's a widget?"

The professor, in an angry tone says, "It's a fictional product, it doesn't matter."

Rodney turns to his son and says, "Doesn't matter??? Tell that to a bank!"

The professor ignores him and turns toward the board and starts to discuss the costs to build a building with rail lines, a shipping dock, etc.

After a few seconds, Rodney pipes up, "Why build? You are better off leasing at a dollar, dollar and quarter or half a square foot. Then take your down payment and put it into CD's or something else you can roll over every couple of months."

The professor says, "Thank you, but we will continue on." The professor then goes on to discuss associated costs with setting up the factory.

After another few seconds Rodney says, "Hold on you left out a bunch of stuff."

The professor says, "Oh really...like what for instance?"

Rodney looks at him smiles and says, "Well first of all, you are gonna have to grease the local politicians for the sudden zoning problems that come up. Then there are the kickbacks to the carpenters...and if you plan on using any cement in the building, I am sure the Teamsters would like to have a little chat with you."

As Rodney begins to talk about this, all of the students turn and start to take notes from him! Rodney goes on, "Don't forget a little something for the building inspectors. Then, there are the long term costs like waste disposal...I am not sure how familiar you are with who runs that business, but I assure you it is not the Boy Scouts!"

At this point, the professor butts in and says, "That will be enough! Maybe these things are how you do business, but they are not part of the legitimate business world!"

The professor then turns back to the board and begins to teach and says, "Disregarding the latest input, the next question is where to build our factory..."

To which you hear Rodney shout from the back of class, "How about Fantasy Land!"

The whole class erupts in laughter.

There is no substitute for real experience. Theory is just that, theory. Until it is put into practice and tested in numerous ways, you do not know if it will work. Reality, no matter what, will always hit you in the face.

Lack of experience leaves you clueless on what to do when reality hits, and when your plan doesn't work. Experience is hard to accelerate since it is an accumulation of learning from being exposed to situations with which you were previously unfamiliar. You can be told about them (as in the humorous "Back to School" story) but nothing replaces the visceral experience of having to deal with unforeseen problems without having "been there, done that" before. That's what the Rodney Dangerfield character was talking about. He had "been there, done that" and knew how things would turn out.

Prior to becoming President, Barack Obama had never run anything, or even been in charge of an organization that was accountable for much of economic consequence. He was an organizer for protests and events, using other people's money. He had spent a few years doing part-time teaching (constitutional law), and after one losing campaign, he was elected to the Illinois State Senate where he racked up an undistinguished record.

His most notable achievement was what he didn't do. He failed to vote—for or against—over 100 bills, simply voting "present," thus leaving no record (to defend). Barack Obama then was hand picked to run for the US Senate (by the Illinois Democratic "machine") and was subsequently elected. He served less than 150 days in the US Senate, yet in that short time, he compiled a voting record as the "most liberal senator" in the Senate. This was in spite of the fact that most of his attention during that time was devoted to preparing for his presidential campaign.

Barack Obama may have endured hardships during his childhood, due to his separated parents and growing up in different places. And yet, after an undistinguished stint at Occidental College, he once again (somehow, mysteriously) was able to get into highly regarded Columbia University. From there, again after a dubious academic record, (somehow, mysteriously) he was able to get into the vaunted Harvard Law School, where he gained his one prestigious post—as the first black editor of the Harvard Law Review, where he "supervised" a staff of 80 editors. Anyone who has attempted to "supervise" lawyers and writers/editors realizes what kind of "supervisory" experience this was—an insignificant one at best.

How Obama kept getting these mysterious advancements, where the funding came from, and what he did to merit them, remains buried in his records, which he maintains sealed from public view to this day. Throughout his career progression, Barack Obama has never had to make tough decisions regarding hiring and firing people, setting goals and plans, helping them earn a livelihood, and learning the lessons of the real world of business, economics and foreign affairs. He simply had never "been there, done that," to gain any substantial leadership experience

Obama's own account lists as foreign policy experience, "living abroad" (as a child) and "traveling abroad" (as young adult). In short, as alluded to earlier, Barack Obama had great "style," because he was educated, unaccented and according to Senate Democrat Leader, Harry Reid, "an articulate black man" (really only half African-American—from his Kenyan father). If asked to list his accomplishments, Obama's were virtually all in the not-for-profit/activist world, where his leadership skills were tied to advocacy and his oratorical style.

Beyond that, Barack Obama lacked any substantial leadership experience in the business world (thus the relevance of this book) and he never led—or managed—an organization of any size. This is not his "fault" per se. It simply explains why there are so many leadership lessons to be learned by the errors and failures in his presidency.

Political professionals managed Obama's presidential campaign, arguably a very well run effort. In virtually all of the essential skills and experience areas to manage an immense responsibility such as the Presidency of the most influential country in the world, Barack Hussein Obama had none of them.

This has been evident throughout his presidency, with Obama shying away from big decisions and seldom seizing the opportunity to lead and/or to govern. The debt ceiling debate was just one notable example of this. Obama stayed out of it and went golfing or on vacation, until he absolutely had to get involved in the final hours and even then, he did not do much. He resorted to his petulant, frustrated, scolding demeanor, ultimately storming out of one critical session after a failed attempt to renegotiate a "done deal." Then he made a speech—or two.

Another example of his leadership and managerial failure is President Obama's budgeting—or lack thereof. At this point, 3+ years into his Presidency, Obama has yet to pass a budget, which is one of the President's primary duties. This responsibility was not helped by the Democrat controlled Congress of 2008-2010, which failed to send the president a budget for the entire two years. In the words of Congressman Charlie Rangel, answering Bill O'Reilly's question as to why not, "We just never got around to it."

In fact, the one budget proposal that President Obama did send to Capitol Hill, in February 2011, was ludicrous. It was even voted down resoundingly by the Democrat controlled Senate. That's right, the Senate members from his own party, failed to vote for it. Why? Because it was, as Rodney Dangerfield would have put it, "in Fantasy Land!" That budget proposed spending $1.40 for each $1.00 of incoming revenue, elevating budget deficits to new record highs. Yet this is the path he is leading America down—annual deficits of over $1 trillion for each year of his presidency.

There is an important lesson in this failure. No entity can continue to spend far in excess of its revenue (income) indefinitely without serious adverse consequences. Clearly President Obama has never learned this lesson

The latest example of Obama's lack of business acumen was in allowing his Energy Department to guarantee loans for hundreds of millions of dollars to "alternative energy" companies that could not get private market support. This was not only Solyndra[5] but

---

5 The Government Accountability Office has been highly critical of the way guaranteed loans and grants were doled out by the Department of Energy, complaining that the process appears "arbitrary" and lacks transparency. In March 2011, for example, the GAO examined the first 18 loans that were approved and found that none were properly documented. It also noted that officials "did not always record the results of analysis" of these applications. A loan program

also many others, some of which are now in the process of failing, which will cost American taxpayers hundreds of millions of dollars more!

Is it a coincidence that the heads of these companies were financial supporters of the Obama campaign and frequent guests at the White House? Perhaps not. Since there were so many such questionable loan guarantees and examples of "crony capitalism" rather than list them all over and over, we will refer to them as "Solyndra type" (or "Solyndra, et. al.").

The president has proven that he cannot lead the country, nor manage the duties of the presidency on theories, nor can he get results based on "hope." You cannot manage a business, a team, or successful organization on theories or on hope either. If you are in a position of leadership (or aspire to be in one) you must gain the necessary experience and knowhow to perform in that position. There is no quick way to do this! Gaining experience takes time and effort. The only place that "success" comes before "work" is in the dictionary. You must be willing to take the time and make the effort, to learn what you need to know, so that you can manage well and lead effectively.

How do you get the experience? First, study other great leaders throughout time, and learn from what they did. Next, seek out mentors who have done what you aspire to do, and learn from their wisdom and experience. Finally, seek out the right mentors and advisors within and outside of your organization, people that have been successful at doing what you want to do, and ask them to share with you how they did it.

---

for electric cars, for example, "lacks performance measures." No notes were kept during the review process, so it is difficult to determine how loan decisions were made.

The GAO further declared that the Department of Energy "had treated applicants inconsistently in the application review process, favoring some applicants and disadvantaging others." The Department of Energy's inspector general, Gregory Friedman, who was not a political appointee, chastised the alternative-energy loan and grant programs for their absence of "sufficient transparency and accountability." He has testified that contracts have been steered to "friends and family." http://www.thedailybeast.com/newsweek/2011/11/13/how-obama-s-alternative-energy-programs-became-green-graft.html

At some point, you will be ready for the leadership position that you aspire to. No matter what, you will always have new things to learn, but you can certainly prepare yourself by acquiring the right skills and knowledge to be successful before taking on the role. Don't pretend to be ready when you are not, or as stated earlier in the chapter, reality will hit you in the face. Hard!

OBAMA PRESIDENCY BACKGROUND AND TYPICAL ISSUES

Facts chronicling Barack Obama's lack of experience in executive leadership and in management are so numerous that most readers know about them. Having been chosen the first black editor of the Harvard Law Review seems to he one of his seminal achievements (where he "supervised" a staff of 80 editors). Much of his career experience was as a community organizer and/or an informal leader of protest efforts (at Harvard). It is unclear whether or where he ever managed a substantial number of people or a sizable budget.

In Chicago, Obama worked as a civil rights attorney and taught Constitutional law part time over a twelve-year period. His foreign policy credentials consisted of having lived abroad as a child, and traveled there briefly as an adult. Obama's governmental experience consisted of three terms (1997-2004) in the Illinois Senate (during which time he simply voted "present" on over 100 bills, and lost an election for a seat in the US House). Obama's term of 143 days in the US Senate was largely spent campaigning for the presidency. Even in this brief Congressional stint, his voting record earned him the title of most liberal Senator in 2007.

It is not surprising given his background, that when confronted with what is arguably the biggest, most complex management and leadership job imaginable—president of the United States—Barack Obama had little relevant managerial or executive leadership experience to rely on, with the exception of his legal background and his ability to make rousing speeches.

∽

"It's not what you don't know that gets you; it's what you thought you knew that ain't so."

—*Josh Billings*

CHAPTER EIGHT

YOU ARE ONLY AS GOOD AS THE PEOPLE YOU SURROUND YOURSELF WITH

Leaders are only as good as the people they select to surround them. Success is never a "one person show." Behind every great leader's success is a solid, experienced team helping in all areas that it takes to achieve success. The mark of whether a leader is "good or bad" comes from their ability to select the right people to fulfill the necessary leadership roles, and help them work together as part of an effective organization.

If leaders are not skilled in these areas they will fail. If they are skilled in these areas, then they can become incredibly successful. Why? Ultimately, the leader cannot have all of the answers, or be expert in every area. Leaders must be competent—have a good, sound base of knowledge in each area in which they lead—but their ability to select the right people as experts, to augment their leadership in each area, is critical to their success.

Since being elected president, Barack Obama has struggled in the selection of highly competent people to surround him. Well into the first year of his presidency, he had not even filled all of the key positions in his cabinet and of those people that he did choose to fill these positions; many had little or no real world experience. In Obama's first three years in office, he will have had three different people (plus an interim) occupy the critical role of his Chief of Staff. This, in itself is revealing.

Consider the contrast between President Barack Obama and President Ronald Reagan. Reagan never felt he was the smartest man in the room. He wasn't, in many regards, but he had a remarkable skill for surrounding himself with the right kinds of "smart people"—with knowledge needed to help a troubled country recover as quickly as possible. Reagan was also known to include (and listen to) advisors who held opposing viewpoints to his, not just party loyalists or sycophants.

Most of Obama's administration has been made up of academics with theoretical experience, or career politicians. Only rarely has he "reached across the aisle" for staff help, with a few notable exceptions such as Defense Secretary Gates (retained from the Bush presidency, and now gone), Transportation Secretary LaHood and China Ambassador Jon Huntsman. Many of Obama's picks lacked the leadership skills, the right experience and the overall competence needed for their positions. Others appear to have left in frustration. This is evident by the lack of success in dealing with issues like the economy, where the Obama administration has struggled over the past 3 years. Also notable is the fact that many of Obama's original advisors—especially economic advisors—have left to return to the safe havens of academic or political/consulting careers. Advisors who had those skills, rather quickly became frustrated, disenchanted and then left (most recently, Chief of Staff Bill Daley).

If you want to be successful, you must have the ability to select the right team to support the vision and mission, and align their efforts to succeed. And you must be open to, and listen to honest feedback and dissenting viewpoints. This is critical to your success. In fact, your ability in this area may be the most important skill you must develop.

What can you do to make sure that you are successful in picking the right people for your team? First, define clearly what kind of talent and experience you are seeking. What does the job require? Then take the time to learn how to interview and select candidates. It is sad, but many times a leader will interview someone for a brief time (an hour or so) for a very important position, during which the leader is talking half of the time, explaining or selling the job to the interviewee. At the conclusion of this interview, if it "goes well," they will decide to hire the person. The question this raises is, "How well can they really get to know and evaluate someone in an hour or two?"

Think about it. How do you determine if their values line up with yours, and your team, and your vision? How do you know they will fit your team's culture? How do you assess their overall competency? How do you know that they have the right capabilities to excel in the position?

A good interviewing and recruiting/screening process will help you answer these questions. Elements of such a process include: a clear definition of the job and its requirements; pre-screening before the interview to determine whether the person should even be interviewed; multiple interviews with specific topics covering the skillsets, experience and values you want in a team member; interviews with current team members to make sure there is a culture fit; contacts with past employers, checking references thoroughly; and that's just a partial list.

The newly elected Obama administration was swamped with applicants, but the vetting process quickly found many to be willing and enthusiastic, but unqualified or otherwise unsuitable (e.g., for background or legal reasons). We wonder how well they were screened for providing different perspectives.

Another useful skill to help in selecting the right team is to build strong networks of trusted people that you can rely on to help find candidates. You should always look for "A players," which are people that are in the top 5-10% of available candidates. Do not compromise just to "get a body in a seat."

A great example is provided by Zappos. If you have never read about Zappos' interview process, take some time to research it. Remember, Zappos is an online shoe retailer—that's it—just shoes. It has been incredibly successful because its employees are fanatical about working there and servicing clients. In fact, it has a very lengthy interview process and if you are selected as a candidate for hire, it actually offers you $4000 to "go away" at the end of the first year. That is how the company truly tests how badly someone wants to work there and be a part of the Zappos culture.

Organizations also quickly take on the character and culture of the leaders. Leaders' behaviors are rapidly observed and imitated—both good and bad ones. An organization tends to reflect the culture and standards set by its leaders, in both ethics and performance. A wise man once said, "Eagles don't flock, but turkeys do—and so do vultures." Another pitfall is when the people in an organization are all similarly capable—but not "A players"—they can settle into a comfortable, self-serving mediocrity. Unless outside disturbances move it out of its comfort zone, it deludes itself into an illusion of success—in spite of external indications to the contrary.

Reflect on the lessons from President Obama's staffing mistakes and near misses. Take time and care in your selection and interviewing process. Know what you need. Select only the best (preferably experienced) candidates, those who are in the top 5-10% of competency in the area of your need. Then make sure they are (or can quickly become) "fanatical" about your culture and vision. As the old adage says, "Be slow to hire and quick to fire [misfits and incompetents]."

OBAMA PRESIDENCY BACKGROUND AND TYPICAL ISSUES

As President, Barack Obama chose a staff on which private sector experience is almost non-existent. In doing this, his organization reflects and reinforces his own lack of experience and reliance on theory, politics and persuasion. Thus the advice he gets about how to deal with a failing economy is at best theoretical and at worst, ineffective—but always consistent with what he thinks/believes.

The difficulty of filling some staff positions was worsened by withdrawals due to problems (tax avoidance and other misbehaviors) of the candidates. In fact, Obama's current Treasury Secretary Geithner had to retroactively remedy income tax evasion issues. Former Congressman Tom Daschle was an early Obama pick for a cabinet position that withdrew rather than face scrutiny of the review process.

Some of Obama's best advisors on the campaign trail (e.g., Former Fed chairman Paul Volcker) did not stay with his advisors once he was elected. Some of Obama's claimed achievements in foreign policy have been as a result of retaining the same people his predecessor, George W. Bush had in place (SecDef Gates). Many people consider Obama's smartest appointment to be that of Hillary Clinton—his vehement primary competitor—to the Secretary of State position. Clinton supporters wonder if this was part of a plan to keep Hillary "out of town" and further from the White House and Washington political visibility.

༄

"The only difference between a tax man and a taxidermist is that the taxidermist leaves the skin."

—Mark Twain

༄

CHAPTER NINE

You Are Known by the Company You Keep

The last chapter and this one differ significantly. Picking a business team is one thing, but choosing who you surround yourself with, both inside and outside of your work life, can have a great effect on your success, your beliefs, your behaviors, and the direction of your life. The views, values, ways of thinking, and perceptions of those you choose to associate with will ultimately "rub off" on you.

Don't believe it? Think about it. From the time you are born, the influences surrounding you help shape you and your life. Parents, teachers, friends, media, culture, religion, etc. and their influences have all shaped who you are up to this point. How many things do you do because, "That's the way I was taught." or "That's how my parents did it."

Just because you were taught to do things a certain way or believe certain things does not always mean that they were (or are) correct, or even the best way. This is a tough realization, but ultimately you are a product of life influences and those influences, good and bad, can help or hinder your success and leadership ability.

"Dirt rubs off on you, and you can't scrub it off," no matter how hard you try. You only get one reputation and one chance to make a first impression. Don't waste these chances. During adolescence, we call choosing bad people to associate with as "running with the wrong crowd"—the malcontents, the rabble-rousers or the under-achievers. At other times, the reverse is true. In college, it's common for a group to form made up of elit-ists—people who feel they are clearly superior to others—and act that way. In either case, being with the "wrong company" infects a person with the flaws in their behavior or character—sometimes incurably.

President Obama has amassed a long list of negative influences in this area, and he does everything possible to avoid admitting the obvious effects of these influences.

- It is a fact that in his formative years Barack Obama was closely tied to Frank Marshall Davis an avowed communist and socialist.
- It is a fact that one of Obama's early associations was with Saul Alinsky, Marxist author of _Rules for Radicals_
- It is a fact that Barack Obama spent many years in Reverend Jeremiah Wright's church listening to angry, black libera-tion theology.
- It is a fact that Obama also had considerable contact with Bill Ayers, the former head of the "Weather Underground," an anti-US socialist organization that bombed the Pentagon, and perhaps Bernadette Dorn too, also of that organization.
- It is a fact that the Obama home in Chicago was acquired in a questionable series of "friendly transactions," involving convicted Chicago mobster Antoin "Tony" Rezko.
- And he was raised in a Muslim country (Jakarta, Indonesia) in his early years, age 6-10—which could be a potential explanation for his current Muslim sympathies.
- But this is just a partial list…from Obama's formative years.

Even in Barack Obama's memoirs, (which many think Ayers heavily contributed to "ghost writing") he states that he intentionally sought out the radicals to spend time with during his early life and while in college. In short, much of Barack Obama's life was spent around radicals, dissidents, and socialist/Marxist thinkers, learning from these people and absorbing their belief systems. How would you imagine his belief systems would develop?

But, President Obama then spends much of his time either denying these facts or shying away from them. Why? It is our view that he does so because he knows that if his true positions were really known, and his true values and influences were really put in the spotlight, he would not be looked upon favorably by a country in which the majority of people do not share such thinking. Thus he has to deny or hide his life influences and beliefs from the American people.

The problem Obama encounters is that eventually many of these conditioned traits, influences, and beliefs are revealed by his behavior and ideology. As his presidency has progressed, this has happened more and more. It is evident when he says things like "we must fundamentally change America." The issue many Americans have with this is embodied in two basic questions: Why, and how?

The fundamental basis of America is the Constitution. Why does it need to be changed, after guiding America for over 200 years? The U.S. has produced more prosperity and human growth in its relatively short time in existence—just over 200 years—than any other civilization. Why does that need to be changed, and how?

Barack Obama demonizes the rich and resorts to class warfare, just as Karl Marx detailed in his teachings. Obama criticizes heartland American people with statements about them like, "[they] cling to their guns and religion," but only says it in front of a small group of like-minded supporters. Or so he thought; the camera, microphone, and video recorder are always on it seems. Then he goes out and campaigns in those areas on those very issues as if he has the same beliefs they do. This is moral and intellectual dishonesty unworthy of the leader of the country. Americans are beginning to see this more and more.

President Obama also chose to surround himself with people—inside and outside his administration—like Van Jones, an avowed Communist, and Cass Sunstein (one of his many czars) who seems to support forced sterilization. Obama has people in his cabinet that make statements like, "we believe like Mao, that all power comes from the barrel of a gun." This is just wrong.

When you look at the countless facts, Barack Obama does not surround himself with people that are passionate about the United States, or reflect the mainstream values on which the country is founded. Instead he surrounds himself with those that represent the antithesis of those values and fundamentals.

The lesson here is starkly obvious. You must choose carefully whom you spend your time with and make sure that they are truly consistent with your values, beliefs, mission, and vision. As a leader, you cannot hide these beliefs and values—at least not for long.

Ask yourself about the people you spend time with, "Is being with this person helping me or hurting me?"   If it is the latter, distance yourself from them. It is only a matter of time before they reflect badly upon you, and it becomes apparent to those around you who and what you really are. Sooner or later, you will be judged by the company you keep.

OBAMA PRESIDENCY BACKGROUND AND TYPICAL ISSUES

Barack Obama's early associates were an infamous group of well-known radicals, revolutionaries, and questionable characters such as Obama's long-time pastor in Chicago, Jeremiah Wright, who was a militant, outspoken and controversial influence—one that Obama quickly disassociated himself from—but only after Wright's incendiary sermons received wide video exposure.. This list is long, but the group already mentioned suffices to illustrate the nature of "the company he kept."

෴

"The government cannot give to anybody anything that the government does not first take from somebody else."

CHAPTER TEN

STAY HUMBLE, DON'T BELIEVE YOUR OWN HYPE

Whoever says "I" the most usually doesn't win in the long run. There is no "I" in "TEAM." It's lonely when you are wrong, and there are few situations where the leader of an organization actually does the successful work. Ideally, the leader develops a plan, assigns talent, obtains resources and assures that a sound strategy and execution are followed. Then the leader's job is to keep things on track.

The best leaders are humble, "servant leaders"[6] who see their role as one of supporting and enabling the organization to succeed. Alone, the leader can do very little. When success happens, the best leaders take less than their share of the credit and when there is a failure they take more than their share of the blame.

Humility is becoming a very scarce quality in our media obsessed society. Everyone wants to be in the spotlight, President Obama included. Have you ever noticed how much of the time Barack Obama spends saying "I" did this, or alternatively, stepping

---

6   Greenleaf, Robert. *Servant Leadership.* Paulist Press. 1977.

back and blaming others for problems or failures. The problems are never his fault or his mistake. It is always someone else's error or omission.

Obama, in a hubris-filled session on CBS 60-Minutes, said that he… "…has not made a wrong decision in his presidency." He also seldom gives credit to those around him for their efforts. It always comes back to him; what he decided, what he did, or what he is going to do or has done.

No person is an island. Neither is anyone omniscient. No one is all knowing or all-powerful (except for Divine beings). You must practice humility and allow others to be recognized and rewarded for their efforts in helping you achieve success. When you lead, it is not about you; it is about them (your team, your shareholders, your customers, etc.).

You cannot be successful long-term by neglecting those that make you a success—or worse yet, taking credit for what they accomplished. President Obama is beginning to encounter this now, as more and more of his initial supporters—the ones that helped elect him—are distancing themselves from him, disenchanted with how they see him behave. This is especially true of many independent voters.

As a leader, you must devote the time to recognize and reward people where credit is due, lifting them up and inspiring or encouraging them, even standing behind them when they have tried to do the right things but failed or done wrong. You must make them part of something bigger than themselves, and let them help to shape and share a role in that greater vision. People will support what they help to create much more enthusiastically than when told what they should or must do.

A great leader helps people to reach levels that they may not think possible for them to recognize and reach their true potential; and then helps them achieve that potential. This can only be done by truly being committed to people, making it about them and their success; this is what a "servant leader" does.

If you find yourself taking more than your share of the credit, think hard about ways that you can allow others to share in the "win" and "spotlight." It not only helps you "win" as well, but it also builds a more devoted and loyal group of supporters.

OBAMA PRESIDENCY BACKGROUND AND TYPICAL ISSUES

President Barack Obama, in addition to making more televised speeches than any other president has used the pronouns "I" and "My" in his speeches far more than any other president. Speaking experts also cite Obama's speaking techniques as unusually effective as a result of using a series of near-hypnotic forms of phraseology that have proven persuasive power. No wonder he holds himself in such high regard. He has hypnotized himself into believing that he does know it all, and is always right—"the smartest person in any room."

∽

"It is one of the most beautiful compensations of this life that no man can sincerely try to help another without helping himself."

—*Ralph Waldo Emerson*

∽

CHAPTER ELEVEN

BEWARE THE PRETENDER

R emember: reality will always hit you in the face—and it hurts. America's current problems are not all George W. Bush's fault. It's that simple. No matter how many times President Obama refers to the "problems he inherited," he has now been in office three years. Certainly many of the current problems can be traced back to events that happened during the eight years that Bush held the top office, and some can be traced back to even earlier presidencies—but far from all of them.

Many of the problems are newly created (or made worse), and Barack Obama owns them. Candidate Obama stepped up and essentially said, "I want the job, and everything that comes with it" by running for president. After three years in office, the problems now belong to him and his presidency. He caused them, made them worse, or didn't solve them. Either way, they are his now.

Just as in any family, company, or organization, those that choose to lead and take on that role must be accountable for it—and everything that comes with it. In leadership, you cannot "pretend" to be a leader. You either are—or you aren't—a leader. One or the other will become apparent very quickly.

If you want the leadership job, you must step up and take full ownership of it. A "pretender" or "poser" is like an actor who has learned all the right lines, but has no idea what they mean. Once the script has been followed (or deviated from), the actor is clueless about what to do next. In theater, a director calls the shots and directs the action. In business, there is no director, per se. This is the job of the leader. Unfortunately, in this government, the "directors" often seem clueless, having learned in academia where results and wins/losses are theoretical, or in politics where success (at getting elected) is more a matter of rhetoric than results.

If you are not ready for a position, or do not believe that you have what it takes to rise to the challenge (or clean up the mess even if you believe it is not your mess), then do not take the job. This was Barack Obama's fundamental mistake. He grossly underestimated the difficulty of the position he was running for, and overestimated his preparedness to actually do the job. Just because he could "talk a good game" (thanks to a phalanx of speech writers and the omnipresent teleprompters) does not mean he actually knew what to do or how to do it. The presidency of the United States of America is not a place for heavy OJT (On-the Job-Training).

Obama's perceived preparedness for the presidency is a terrible delusion, from which it is difficult to escape. Mistakes build upon each other and result in even more complex problems. Difficult problems that are mishandled become even more difficult to fix. When you have too little experience, lack substance (other than the words of your latest speech), then leading, managing and problem solving simply don't happen. And that is what has occurred. When you compound the problem by surrounding your self with like-minded theorists, lacking in real-world experience, things become worse yet. The theoretical solutions to problems often don't work due to the messiness of the real world—and the reasons are almost unfathomable to these rookie executive/politicians.

Imagine for a moment a metaphorical scenario. Jeffrey Immelt, the President's Jobs Council Chairman, is Chairman of the Board of Directors and Chief Executive Officer of an immense multi-national company, General Electric. He was given that job after nearly three decades of successful performance at different levels and in different divisions of GE. During these years, Immelt learned from many leaders. (Not the least of which was his notable predecessor, Jack Welch). He gained experience from many different situations and proved his readiness to ultimately become Chairman and CEO.

Now imagine that Immelt is looking for a successor. There is a promising young manager in one of GE's divisions, currently working 3-4 organizational levels below the CEO spot. This man (or woman) is bright, articulate, and highly regarded, and has been successful in his/her short stints—two jobs—with GE—in just a few years time.

In a corporate setting, this person would be termed "high potential." Development plans would be charted, discussed, and then implemented. The plan would be to prepare the person for a senior executive position in 10-15 years or so. Maturity, in age, is also a critical part of experience, in preparation for a difficult, complex job.

Now suppose that this high potential person was asked to speak at a large corporate meeting, as part of the management development process. Having prepared well to speak on a narrow and familiar topic, and being a bright and articulate person (and a minority too!), this aspiring manager "wows" the audience, which consists of GE's senior and mid-level management. Would they consider for a moment, jumping this high potential person over 3-4 levels of management and installing him/her as Immelt's successor?

Of course not. The very idea is preposterous. And yet, that is exactly what happened to catapult Barack Obama into the Presidency of the United States of America. He "played the role" for a few brief moments, on the big stage at the 2004 Democratic National Convention, and he was "fast tracked" all the way into the White House.

To this very day, he "plays the role" of President quite well, as long as the performance can be tightly scripted, and the decisions involved are not too difficult or complex. That's why Obama prefers to campaign instead of governing; to make a speech instead of making policy; to blame failures on his predecessors, his opponents, and his staff. He couldn't possibly have done anything wrong—"it wasn't in the script." Unfortunately, as we have said before, "reality will hit you in the face"—and it hurts.

Resolve not to pretend to be the right person for the role, just because it seems glamorous. You will find that for every bit of glamour, there is 10 times more challenge and responsibility than you imagined. Beware of people you recognize as "pretenders," because they are very destructive, usually most harmful to those closest to them. There is nothing worse than someone who thinks they know everything, but actually has no clue, and does not want to take responsibility for his/her actions and decisions.

Losers (pretenders) make promises, which they break. Winners make commitments, which they keep. Competent executives accept responsibility and accountability. Pretenders talk a good game, but since they are clueless about what to do next, they grasp frantically at a fragmented array of quick fixes or staff proposals and then blame everyone but themselves when things don't work.

OBAMA PRESIDENCY BACKGROUND AND TYPICAL ISSUES

Why does Barack Obama use the Teleprompter so much? It is the only way he can communicate both effectively and concisely, relying on the expertise of his speech writing staff and his own "style" of delivery. When he must speak or answer questions extemporaneously, Obama's delivery is lengthy, wandering, punctuated with pauses and clearly not that of the articulate "performer" he is when using his Teleprompters.

❧

"We hang the petty thieves and appoint the great ones to public office."

—Aesop

❧

III
TRUTH AND CONSEQUENCES

"Say what you mean, and mean what you say."

CHAPTER TWELVE

WORDS AND HOW YOU USE THEM ARE POWERFUL

How many times have you seen someone put their proverbial "foot in their mouth?" How many times have you seen a career or enterprise ruined just because of something someone said? Words and how you use them are very powerful.

Be careful you don't say what you really didn't mean to say—and that you do say what you intended to say. One of the cardinal sins in politics is when a politician accidentally blurts out "the whole truth," when that was not what was intended. Choose words carefully, because their meaning is interpreted in the minds and from the perspectives of those who hear them. In many cases, it is not just what you say, but how you say it that matters as well—and that includes non-verbal "body language."

A great example of how out of control this has become in today's society happened in October of 2011. The iconic Monday Night Football music theme was dropped, after being used for over a decade, because of one off-hand comment by the singer of theme, Hank Williams Jr. He said that John Boehner playing golf with Obama was like Netanyahu playing golf with Hitler.

OK, so that's a little extreme, even for Hank, but the metaphor—the two people referenced really are polar opposites—was the message Hank likely tried to convey. It didn't matter. His analogy likened Obama to Hitler and that was totally unacceptable. As soon he said it, Hank's fate was sealed. The sad thing is he could have easily used a different example—cats and dogs maybe—but once you start talking about a genocidal madman like Hitler in comparison with a US president, your words will hurt you.

Barack Obama's use of words is also a great case study. He has the ability to use words and how he says them to great advantage, although less so when speaking extemporaneously and not using a Teleprompter. A great example involved the first stimulus package. When the stimulus was passed, the Obama administration said it would "create" millions of jobs and keep the unemployment rate under 8%. When it became apparent that this would not happen, Obama changed the wording to "create <u>or save</u> millions of jobs," and the unemployment rate part just was dropped. That's a big difference in meaning. (Remember Bill Clinton's famous statement, "It depends on what the definition of "is" is..."? That was another example of how powerful words can be—even short ones like "is.")

Words can create false hopes, or destine aspiring hopes to failure. Words can energize or debilitate. Words can lie subtly but certainly, or can tell the truth, delicately or brutally. Words matter. How they are used, matters even more. In many respects the wording used can result in intellectual honesty —or dishonesty. The choice of words can convey intentions far beyond what they actually describe.

President Obama has shown time and time again that his use of words in phrases such as, "fundamentally change America," and "spread a little bit of the wealth around," have much deeper meaning. But they roll so easily off his tongue that few people notice or stop to think about what is he really saying.

Another great example of words and their use involved the "Obamacare" bill as it as being passed by Congress. Almost two-thirds of the American people were against the passage of the bill, but in the late hours of Christmas Eve, House Speaker Nancy Pelosi pushed the bill through by saying, "We have to pass the bill to see what is in it." This is another incredible use of wording, not by President Obama, but by one of his close Democratic allies.

Even the naming of laws can mislead people or cause them to misinterpret the content. By calling "Obamacare" The Patient Protection and Affordable Care Act, it infers that the law does both of these things—and in some parts, it does. In other parts, it does just the opposite, taking substantial funding away from patients and making health care less affordable and/or reducing patient protection (e.g., Medicare cuts).

The Employee Free Choice Act, which was defeated by Congress, would have taken away employees' right to secret ballot union elections, thus denying them one part of their "free choice"—privacy of the ballot box. In fact, all political maneuvering uses words to deceive and/or to persuade. It is just the fact that Barack Obama's presidency has raised this to the level of a fine art; especially via the President's articulate contradictions, as he tries to please as many constituents as possible.

As a leader, you must learn to use the power of what you say and how you say it to your advantage. Pay very careful attention to what you say. There are many constituents in any audience. Whether they read or hear the words, each processes them with the filter, "what does this mean to me?" Then they use the second filter: "what does this mean I must do, or not do, believe, or accept, or not?"

This can work both positively and/or negatively for you. If you have bad intentions, then words can be used to mask those intentions, and get what you want, even if it hurts others in the process. But, if you have good intentions, the things you say—and how you say them—can create good and help others. Words can get people involved in a vision, and energize them—or not. You can accomplish amazing things by choosing the right words.

Think about how something you say might impact the various parts of your audience before saying it. Think about what you want your overall message to be, and how you want it to be perceived. Pay careful attention to inflection and how you emphasize points, and when (in your remarks) you make those points. Pay attention to your non-verbal body language too. Learn the vocabulary and culture of your audience so that you can make sure to truly identify and communicate with them—just make sure you stick to your core values and don't "pander to your audience." As a leader, your ability to deliver a message and incite action as a result of your message will play a major part in your organization's success.

OBAMA PRESIDENCY BACKGROUND AND TYPICAL ISSUES

President Obama's use of "hypnotic phrasing techniques" adds to the effect of his choice of words. This allows him to "parse the truth" and reduce outright lies to simple "misstatements," which can be more easily glossed over by his "spin doctors." To further complicate matters, within the same speech, President Obama will make contradictory statements with such effortless phrasing that both sound credible and even logical. For example, only the more astute members of the audience can connect statements about the need to reduce spending and deficits with later statements about the need to continue to invest (spend) on numerous programs.

Barack Obama's choice of words, contextual phrasing and timing (separation) make illogical and contradictory statements seem consistent and acceptable. Words truly are powerful for this president.

৩৯

"Government is the great fiction, through which everybody endeavors to live at the expense of everybody else."

—Frederic Bastiat, (French economist 1801-1850)

৩৯

CHAPTER: THIRTEEN

BE PREPARED TO DEAL WITH THE CONSEQUENCES OF YOUR ACTIONS

Accountability is a word that seems to have less and less importance in society today. It has become very easy to escape responsibility by pointing the finger at someone else or giving excuses as to why something did not work. When it comes to someone's actions, it is hard for them to not be held accountable because what they do can be tracked, seen, measured, and critiqued.

Your actions will speak louder than your words, and lead to many consequences—some of which you will expect—or to unintended consequences. People around you are constantly observing what you do and comparing that to their expectations, most of which you have created by what you said or did in the past. The way you choose to act will have a huge impact on your ability to lead, your level of success, and ultimately the perception of everyone around you. Even more important is how you react to the consequences of your actions.

Barack Obama has proven that he does not want to deal with the consequences of his actions and has done everything possible to distance himself from many of his actions as they have become unpopular. Examples abound, including his handling of the budget, and the many promises he made both as a candidate and a president that have either never happened or were miserable failures (Closing Guantanamo is a just one of the best examples). Whatever the action, Obama has had a hard time taking responsibility for and dealing with the consequences, and his constituents are noticing it more and more. Conversely, he desperately holds to other accountabilities (e.g., exiting Iraq) with less than appropriate concern about the unintended consequences.

When you lead, you must take full responsibility for the actions that you take, and be prepared to work through any consequences of your decisions. Those around you, especially your subordinates, will watch everything you do as a leader. Maybe that is why it has been said that many times an employee doesn't leave a company or an organization, they leave the leader. This happens in many cases because the leader has failed the person that is leaving. You must strive to never fail those around you in this way. Always be conscious of your actions and the impact they will have on the people around you.

The laws of physics apply to so much of life, that this case is no exception. One such law states, "For every action there is an equal and opposite reaction." Barack Obama's desperate "class warfare" speeches to force his agenda onto the American people (e.g., the latest "Jobs Bill") are creating both unintended consequences and predictable reactions.

An unintended consequence is manifesting itself as the "Occupy..." movement. Even if sympathetic to part of the "Occupy..." cause, most responsible Americans are alarmed by the extreme nature of many protesters in the movement. While some participants have rightful concerns, many more are rabble-rousers or anarchists—disorderly, unlawful and distasteful. Earlier chapters covered the topic of being judged by the company you keep. President Obama is in perilous territory when he chooses to side with the "Occupy..." movement.

Inevitably there are times when things go wrong—even when nothing was done wrong. Thus it's not fair to blame the president for everything that goes wrong. That applies whether his name is Bush or Obama. However, most actions and decisions at this level have consequences, and some of them are unintended, unexpected or both.

How you deal with these consequences is the litmus test of a leader's character, courage and competence. The mark of an experienced leader is to have thought through the most likely consequences and have plans ready on what to do if (or when) unintended consequences occur. Less experienced leaders will make the mistake of being unprepared for adverse outcomes, or try to treat symptoms instead of the root causes of the problems. This generally make things worse, not better. As Abraham Lincoln so aptly put it, "Give me six hours to chop down a tree and I will spend the first four sharpening the axe."

The primary lesson here is that narcissistic leaders seldom blame themselves for the real or unintended consequences of their actions and behavior. Responsible leaders of character, courage and competence take responsibility and accountability for the consequences—whether they are intended or not. If you want the right to make important decisions, you must be prepared to be accountable for the results and outcomes—and take the responsibility for the consequences of decisions. A wise man once advised: "Make reversible decisions quickly; make irreversible decisions slowly." When it comes to dealing with consequences, this is very sound advice.

OBAMA PRESIDENCY BACKGROUND AND TYPICAL ISSUES

One of the most common ways to avoid dealing with the consequences of actions is to "play the victim," as in the President's frequent reliance on statements about what a difficult situation he inherited. Thus, President Obama frequently seems guilty of three common faults of a victim, as described by T. Harv Eker in his book, Secrets of the Millionaire Mind: Justifying: People will rationalize and justify their situation or why they are not where they want to be any way they can. Blame: People will blame *everyone and everything…except themselves, for why they are where they are. <u>Complaining</u>: They complain and focus on the negativity in their lives and that is what they get from it…negative results.*

∽

"If anything can go wrong, it will."

—Murphy's First Law

∽

CHAPTER FOURTEEN

WHEN YOU DON'T HAVE THE ANSWER, DON'T TRY TO SOUND LIKE YOU DO

You can always tell when people don't know what they are talking about. They talk a lot more, have trouble conveying the message of their topic, and continue to go on and on, finally confusing those that are listening. Many times what they say sounds good at first, but they never really get to the point.

When you don't know the answer, it's OK to say, "I don't know, but I'll find out"—unless it's an answer you were supposed to know. Then you have big trouble. Nobody can know everything. To think you do is the height of arrogance, and a precursor to a big fall.

Barack Obama has made a lot of speeches...a lot of speeches! Many times, especially when he is not using a teleprompter, he doesn't have the answer, so he just pontificates until he feels he has talked around the topic enough, even though he never answers the question. Recall the speech where he was tripping over his words talking about getting someone "some treatment" and a "breathalyzer" and he then said "inahlater", "then finally, inhaler." Obama went on to pontificate further for several minutes with no real point, to cover up the fact that he did not know what he was talking about.

He does the same thing when it comes to difficult issues, such as his speech about his latest Jobs Plan. He just kept saying, "Pass this bill." He didn't ask Congress to look at it, or to read it and or to think about it. He just demanded that they "pass it." It was like he forgot how our system of government works, and by saying "pass this bill" over and over again, he could hide the fact that the bill really had very little merit upon which to pass and few good solutions in it. In fact, it took weeks before a Democrat would even sponsor it, to bring the jobs bill to the floor, and that happened because Republicans said they would willingly sponsor it just to get the vote to defeat it over with!

When you work in business or are in any position of leadership, you must not make up things to hide the fact that you do not know the answer. If it is something you just don't know; that may be ok. The key is to know with certainty what you do know—and what you don't know (especially if that can hurt you) and where you can learn it the fastest way.

Let whoever is asking know that you will find out the answer—and then go do it. Go get that answer you didn't know, and use it wisely. If it is an answer that you should know and be prepared with, make sure you do know the answer and are prepared to answer. Only you know what you are responsible for and what you need to know in your business.

Do your homework—always. Make sure that you are always prepared and think through your answers ahead of time, especially if you are going into important meetings (such as those with your superiors or with your customers). The same thing holds true if you must have a critical/difficult conversation with a subordinate or peer. Know what you are going to say, why you are going to say it, and most importantly make sure that you can deliver what you need to say in a clear and concise manner.

When you have said what you planned to say—and what needed to be said—shut up! The more you ramble on, the more likely you will either wander off message, or come across as if you really don't know what you intended to cover—and more importantly—needed to say.

OBAMA PRESIDENCY BACKGROUND AND TYPICAL ISSUES

The president's legal background shows when he is asked something he clearly doesn't know the answer to. He obfuscates, pontificates and eventually migrates to a change of the subject—to something that he does know about. You will also notice him stammer and say "uh" a lot. Thus his answers often resemble "mini-filibusters." But they sure sound good.

∽

"Just because you do not take an interest in politics doesn't mean politics won't take an interest in you!"

—Pericles (430 B.C.)

∽

CHAPTER FIFTEEN

TAKE RESPONSIBILITY FOR YOUR ACTIONS—AND YOUR MISTAKES

Hopefully your parents have told you since you were a child that you should take responsibility for what you do, and live with the consequences of your decisions. While this is age-old advice you've heard before, it is astounding at how many people do not follow it—especially politicians!

Examples of this don't just come from President Obama, but from politicians on both sides of the aisle. Although, it seems more and more nowadays to be worse than it has ever been in Washington. No one, especially President Obama, wants to take responsibility for anything getting done.

As a wise mentor once reminded, "Success has many fathers... but failure is an orphan." This statement is sad, but true. Any time there is success people find every way they can to make themselves a part of it. As soon as they sense they are part of a failure, they try to distance themselves and look for a scapegoat as fast as possible.

Great leaders don't do this. They take responsibility and accept accountability for the results. They also give credit where it is due, in the case of success, and are usually the ones taking the responsibility, in the case of failure. That is probably why they are in leadership positions. The few great leaders who do behave this way—taking on responsibility at the right time, and in the right way—stand out from the crowd.

Don't try the old "look what you made me do" complaint either. It just doesn't work. Own your decisions and actions. Own up to your mistakes and fix them. Even a wrong decision creates the beginning of corrective action. If a person wants to avoid all mistakes, s/he simply makes no decisions and does nothing—and yet, inaction is a decision too.

A good way to see this is to read annual reports of companies that are not doing well and concentrate on the message from the CEO. You can learn as much from what is not said in an annual report as from what is said. Problems are often glossed over, or go totally unmentioned. Failures are rationalized away by placing blame elsewhere, if they are mentioned at all.

Companies that typically get turned around, have messages from the CEO that discuss successes, but also detail problems and failures, including what they intend to do about them. Companies that do not get turned around typically have a CEO with a message about all of the good things and their part in them, and little or nothing about what is not working, or has failed. That's a big difference.

To succeed as a leader, you will need to do your homework; enlist the aid of others; then do what you believe is right and take responsibility for the outcome. We have become a country where people want too many rights without accepting responsibilities. It simply doesn't and cannot work that way. Remember the points about "justifying, blaming, and complaining" in the earlier chapters?

To become great, a leader must take responsibility for success, but not deny the responsibility for failure. In fact, it is through failure that people learn, and if they are open to it, they learn the most from their failures. The best leaders take those lessons and use them to build future success. Embrace this concept, because when you do, truly great things can happen.

OBAMA PRESIDENCY BACKGROUND AND TYPICAL ISSUES

The faults of a victim described at the end of Chapter 13 explain well how Barack Obama reacts far too often, so they are repeated here: Justifying: People will rationalize and justify their situation or why they are not where they want to be any way they can. Blame: People will blame everyone and everything…except themselves, for why they are where they are. Complaining: They complain and focus on the negativity in their lives and that is what they get from it…negative results.

ᕬ

"Foreign aid might be defined as a transfer of money from poor people in rich countries to rich people in poor countries."

—Douglas Casey, (Classmate of Bill Clinton at Georgetown University)

ᕬ

CHAPTER SIXTEEN

THERE ARE NO SUCCESSFUL VICTIMS

There are only unsuccessful victims waiting to get caught. You are the only one who truly can control your destiny, your attitude and your future. The article below, entitled "Regaining American Exceptionalism" that D.M. wrote and John contributed to, was published in 2011, on Forbes.com. It speaks to the distressing trends towards accepting the role of a victim, and much more:

"REGAINING AMERICAN EXCEPTIONALISM"

It is sad, but the persevering, winning attitude that has made Americans what we are is on the decline in our society. The earlier generations of Americans from the Revolutionary War, to the Civil War times, to WWII Era Americans had a sense of pride, a sense of winning—at all costs. That may be why, especially in the case of the latter, that they have been called the "Greatest Generation." It may be no coincidence that as that generation has begun to fade from our society, the sense of winning and pride, has faded as well...

What has replaced it and is becoming more prevalent are a sense of entitlement, mediocrity and an extreme fear of failure. This is evidenced by the fact that more and more we see instances of not awarding grades in school, not keeping score in athletic contests, celebrating finishing 4th and lower, and not even deciding winners (and losers) at all.

While this may say sound like a clever way to help boost self-esteem and many times boosting self-esteem has been used as the excuse for the rewarding of mediocrity. It may in fact be contributing to and conditioning us to strive for lower standards, mediocre results and find still more excuses for why people cannot—or more importantly—will not, work to reach their true potential.

In many ways, Excuses have replaced the spirit in the American people.

Too often these days, it is easier to get what you want (or at least feel like it emotionally) by becoming a victim rather than taking the risks and leaving your comfort-zone, to actually achieve more, and strive for something better.

Failure is rejected in our society. Instead it should be embraced and recognized as a rite of passage to a higher-level of achievement. The worst part of this is that low achievement really is becoming the new norm for many in American society. It has become socially acceptable to "play the role" of the victim.

Notice that I said, "play the role." I did not say that people are victims, because 99% of the time they are not. They have a lot of control over their situation, but are unwilling to do what they know must be done...the extra work and sacrifice. As stated previously, it is now easier and has become socially acceptable to just "play the role" of the victim. So what are the clues that someone is "playing the role" of the victim?

> *In his book, Secrets of the Millionaire Mind, T. Harv Eker narrowed them to down to three:*
>
> *Justifying: People will rationalize and justify their situation or why they are not where they want to be any way they can.*
>
> *Blame: People will blame everyone and everything...except themselves, for why they are where they are.*
>
> *Complaining: They complain and focus on the negativity in their lives and that is what they get from it...negative results.*

Perhaps it is not coincidental that we see all three of these exhibited by the leaders of our country—thus making them seem to be "OK." They are not "OK!"

But...the funny thing is that if you asked someone to name a "successful victim," they most likely would have no answer. Yet, many people, some in high places, believe they can become successful through playing the victim role!

The psychology of Americans using excuses as a way to shirk responsibilities is growing in our society. Consider the commonly heard phrases (excuses): "You can't fight the tide," "It is what it is," "We will just have to deal with it, and the granddaddy of them all: "Don't blame me, it's not my fault."

Well, there is still a group of Americans out here that believe we can change this mentality and it starts with one person at a time, beginning with you—and me. We can influence our destiny—and we do, every day, buy our actions and inactions, or decisions and indecision.

So, how do you change—more importantly—help others to change so that we can bring back the American characteristics that made us exceptional?

Requirements for the Rebirth of American Exceptionalism

Leadership

It all starts with the right leadership...and a dose of tough love. We cannot let the "victim mentality" become a victim identity" for those that we can influence. We must recognize the three victim clues and stop them immediately, even if we find ourselves tempted to use one of them. This will be painful to not only us, and also to those we are trying to help, but it is a necessity.

Entrepreneurship

The success of America and the Greatest Generation was built on entrepreneurship, hard work and sacrifices required to find success. In only the 20th century did working for someone on a mass scale become the norm. What most people fail to realize is that we are all unique in our ability to function as an entrepreneur in some area(s) of our lives. Whether we own a business, start a small business on the side while working elsewhere, or champion a cause about which we feel deeply; we all have an ability to tap into our innate entrepreneurial spirit. This spirit—a uniquely American, can-do spirit—must be recognized and reinforced over and over.

Help Yourself and Others to Become Resourceful

Along with tapping into our individual entrepreneurial spirit, we must always look for ways to make ourselves more resourceful. Today many people wait for someone else to take care of things for them. That is why, as I write this, over 50% of Americans receive some form of public support/ assistance. This quickly becomes debilitating to a person and causes them to undervalue their potential.

America initially prospered because Americans had to be resourceful; they had to "find a way," no matter what. Nowadays, with too many things so easily available and the government willing to help us in exchange for a little more of our freedom each and every day, this American resourcefulness has begun to fade. We must remember and teach others not to give up so easily, but to use their mind and talents to "find a way or make a way."

The proliferation of Internet access and instant gratification has worsened this tendency. So much information is instantly, and readily available to help you find anything we need to succeed. However the Internet is both a blessing and curse. It has conditioned us to get whatever we want, right now, whether it is good for us or not, and if we can't, just give up.

At the same time, the Internet offers us an amazing opportunity to be more resourceful than at any other time in our history. It is our responsibility to realize the difference and use the Internet to improve ourselves, what we can do, and not as a waste of time on mindless distractions.

Teach Others to Seek Failure—and Learn from it

We must seek out the lessons learned from failures, upon which to build our future successes. There is nothing wrong with failing. It means we did something, we took a risk; we got out of our comfort zone. It is in failing that we can grow and learn the most. At the same time failure helps to teach us, and demands that we be more resourceful, so that we can find the ways to overcome obstacles and avoid new failures.

Do Not Accept Excuses

We must neither accept excuses, nor provide excuses, for not achieving what we seek—or for falling short. We must learn to have faith in ourselves and resolve to try again. We must accept responsibility at all times for our actions and results, and teach others to do the same. If we truly want to be in control of our own destiny, we must take responsibility for it.

We Must Celebrate the Individual

Americans used to be called "Rugged Individualists." We must learn to celebrate that characteristic again. We must celebrate the ability of the individual, not of the collective, because it is through individuals that truly great things happen. There is no such thing as "collective salvation," because each person finds salvation in his or her own way.

By salvation, I mean a person's own form of success, happiness, and fulfillment. It does not come from a group. Even if our success is as part of a team effort, we are each unique and can never be defined by a label bestowed upon us by others or by being forced into a group or class. Remember this at all times.

The six characteristics above are simple, but are essential to what we are and can become. Many have forgotten them over time, but they are always there. Our job is not only to remember them to guide our daily lives, but to help bring them out in others and foster them every chance we get.

By doing this both individually and with others around us, on each and every day, I believe that we will start to see the changes that we all are looking for so desperately and desire so much.

This article and the lessons it offers could have been titled, "Regaining Leadership and Business Exceptionalism." Strive to make the contents part of your culture and leadership message. When you choose to be a victim, you relinquish control over your fate and your destiny. Whining, complaining and blaming others are symptoms of the disease of "victimitis." It isn't terminal to your life, but it can be to your career. Only you can treat it and remedy it. Will you?

OBAMA PRESIDENCY BACKGROUND AND TYPICAL ISSUES

Ironically, IL Senator Obama started his national political career with a rousing speech for unity, and even as he started his campaign, he sounded, at times, in favor of the concept of American exceptionalism. Sadly, that changed once he was in office. For the majority of Obama's first two years in office, he traveled internationally criticizing the USA and its behaviors; he blamed most of his problems on his predecessor George W. Bush. Now, with an election looming, he has found new scapegoats— the Republican held House, the Congress in general, and most startling of all—the American people. Next, he will attribute blame to either his election opponents or some "class of society" such as "greedy Wall Street bankers." Victims always need someone to blame, and unfortunately this president is no exception.

∾

"Government's view of the economy could be summed up in a few short phrases: If it moves, tax it. If it keeps moving, regulate it. And if it stops moving, subsidize it."

—Ronald Reagan   (1986)

∾

IV
MISTAKES AND MISUNDER-STANDINGS

"The road to hell is paved with good intentions."

CHAPTER SEVENTEEN

NOBLE INTENTIONS DON'T JUSTIFY SCREWING UP

Leaders cannot build their success upon intentions alone. No matter how good (or bad) your intentions, the results and outcomes never lie. Good intentions are just that, intentions. Depending on who is delivering the message, those intentions may be perceived as good or bad. Intentions are seen, as the old saying goes, "In the eye of the beholder." The best of intentions can lead to the worst of disappointments if the leader doesn't convert the intentions into action and successful outcomes.

People, especially President Obama, but also many other politicians will do anything they can to "justify" how their intentions were good or noble. But, as we discussed earlier, they will not take responsibility for the consequences. Here are 5 examples of Barack Obama's failures of good intentions, for which he has yet to apologize.

The Economy: Even after almost 3 years, it is still "inherited." Obama has blamed the malaise in the economy on George W. Bush for about as long as he could. He threw money at the problems—perhaps with the best of intentions (we're giving him the benefit of the doubt), but to no avail. Then he started blaming others: "greedy Wall Street bankers," a "do nothing Congress," multinational companies who refuse to invest shareholders' money in his failing economy, and so on. No matter how good Obama's intentions may have been, he was (and remains) clueless about why the US economy is foundering and what to do about it.

Hint: It is because of excessive and stifling regulations by Obama's minions: EPA, NLRB, CPSC, and on, and on…and because of the high corporate taxes, and continuing uncertainty about "what will happen next" due to the anti-business behavior of the Obama administration—largely based on the President's adversarial attitude toward business. Barack Obama has written that during a brief stint in the private sector, "he felt like a spy behind enemy lines." Is that revealing enough?

Jobs (or lack thereof): A common mistake, evident in the President's many failed "jobs" initiatives is trying to "rush the harvest." When you do the right things, the right outcomes usually follow, but only after a suitable amount of time has elapsed. When you do the wrong things, the wrong outcomes—or no outcomes at all are what follows. After several failures, it should be logical to stop repeating the same errors. It is also human nature to become impatient and try to rush things along. This is especially true when there is an election coming up. However, time is a perishable asset. No amount of money can buy back lost time. No amount of money will make certain things happen faster than is natural and reasonable. For the president to be taking any credit for the little bit of recovery that is occurring is similar to a rooster's crowing that seems to be taking credit for the sun coming up. Left alone, business cycles will occur—but then that is another incomprehensible piece of knowledge to this president and his staff—and he won't let the cycles occur without meddling (to claim credit).

Mother Nature teaches us well, if we will just pay attention. Farmers (and any gardener) learn this lesson from experience. When planting a crop, the prescribed steps must be followed if success is to be the outcome. The crop must be planted, tended, watered, fertilized and weeded—for a period of time—until it germinates, grows and matures, and only then it can be harvested.

Planting ten crops at once won't yield a harvest any faster—just ten times a much—later. This lesson is one that needs to be learned over and over. Throwing money at things will not make them happen faster. (More on this in another chapter.) This President is just on his first time through "Mother Nature's school of hard knocks." He has a lot more learning to do before he can deliver a successful crop—if that time ever comes.

<u>Fast and Furious:</u> Everyone inside the top tier of Obama's administration has claimed ignorance of this drug-dealer/gun-running scandal gone awry. This whole escapade shows either a lack of leadership, a lack of control, or if those in charge actually did not know about the operation, that they were not doing their job. Those responsible should no longer hold office, whether guilty of either gross incompetence or blatant irresponsibility (Attorney General Eric Holder and his staff). (Contrast this to how President Ronald Reagan quickly went on TV and took responsibility for the failed Iran-Contra scandal.) But all we hear about is how the Fast and Furious program had "good intentions"—it was just mismanaged. Holder should have known; if he didn't shame on him. If he knew and didn't stop it, shame on him again. The practice of saying that an initiative had good intentions, but was just mismanaged, seems to reveal a common thread through Obama's presidency. It seems that it's never the policy or ideas that are wrong, it is just that they haven't been administered right or they have not been done long enough yet. It is a very curious characteristic of both liberal policies in general and especially those of the Obama administration.

<u>Solyndra, et. al.</u>[7]: If Barack Obama were an experienced executive or understood the basics of for-profit capitalism this company

---

7   …The 1705 Loan Guarantee Program and the 1603 Grant Program channeled $-billions to all sorts of energy companies. …for alternative-fuel and green-power projects…. At least 10 members of Obama's finance committee, more than a dozen campaign bundlers were big winners. And several politicians who supported Obama struck gold by launching alternative-energy companies and obtaining grants. … According to the DoE's own numbers, in the 1705 loan program, $16.4 billion of $20.5 billion in loans granted as of Sept. 15 went to companies run by or primarily owned by Obama financial backers, bundlers, or large donors to the Democratic Party. http://www.thedailybeast.com/

would have never been granted huge loan guarantees ($500 mil-lion+) with such a risky and questionable business model. In a cor-porate setting Energy Secretary Chu and others in his department would have been fired for making such irresponsible investment decisions, however noble their intentions. Even if you accept the premise that new, developing technologies require taking greater risk in return for commensurately greater rewards, loan guaran-tees to such business enterprises, whose loans could not justify or get private-sector financial support should have been a serious warning. Solyndra is just the most prominent example; others like Range Fuels[8] (GA-based cellulosic ethanol) cost tax payers millions. Its plant was recently sold in a distress sale for $5 million after the government guaranteed loans of around $200 million were "wasted," in another poorly managed investment. Solyndra became the most famous green/renewable energy misadventure, when President Obama was shown proudly praising it—while it was already in the process of failing. This was yet another instance of his naïve hubris and lack of experience that led to American taxpayers footing the bill for bad investments and/or gross mis-management. Making the excuse that Solyndra was just one unfortunate instance, and we need to do it more of these, only emphasizes the mistakes of idealistic, and inexperienced govern-ment officials, and their leader—Barack Obama. Meanwhile, the president blocked drilling for/recovering US oil in numerous locations. Good intentions do not compensate for bad manage-ment and inept leadership.

Spending: Under President Barack Obama the US has run up a larger deficit in 3+ years of his presidency than all of the other presidents before him combined. That is correct—com-bined! Under Barack Obama, for the first two of his three years, with a Democratically controlled Congress; the USA has spent $1.5 trillion dollars more—each year—than it took in in revenue. By the time Obama finishes his first term in office, he will have

newsweek/2011/11/13/how-obama-s-alternative-energy-programs-became-green-graft.html
8 http://online.wsj.com/article/SB10001424052970204257504577153151863776084.html

presided over the creation of $5 trillion in budget deficits, without ever having passed a budget—part of his job! Part of this problem was admittedly a decline in revenue due to the recession. But a larger part of it was uncontrolled spending, which started during the Bush administration/Republican Congress, but accelerated to more than three times the pace of over-spending after Obama took office. And there is no relief in sight.

Example: Government spending in Obama's first two years averaged $3.6 Trillion and Revenue averaged $2.2 Trillion. This amounts to spending almost $1.40 for every $1.00 of revenue— on a continuing basis. The only budget "proposal" submitted— ever—by President Obama was in February of 2011, which called for spending in 2011-2012 of $3.7 Trillion against expected revenue of $2.3 Trillion. Fortunately, this budget was voted down unanimously by the Democrat controlled Senate. Even Obama's own party knew how foolish it was and rejected it.

Yet President Obama keeps justifying his plans to spend more as "investments," but investments have expected returns, whereas his spending simply creates greater and greater deficits. When his plans are rejected, Obama turns petulant and reverts to the class warfare card—vilifying the "millionaires and billionaires" for not paying their fair share (or by having VP Joe Biden threaten that if the House blocks more spending, "there will be more rapes!") Note: If the government took ALL of the income of the "millionaires and billionaires" in taxes, it wouldn't even cover one year of Obama deficits. How sad is that?

VP Joe Biden: Joe Biden is the perfect example of not choosing strength, but rather choosing for political expedience. (You don't hear anyone talking about Biden being a viable successor to Obama. They know that is just wrong.) Biden had a long and distinguished Senate career—and as such, he fit the criteria for a good running mate for the rookie Obama. But since his choice to be VP, Biden has done and said the most outrageous things. Not only do his actions and what he says, often make reasonable people shake their heads in dismay, but the frightening fact is that Obama believed he was the right person to be next in line for the presidency. Judging by decisions like that one, you must question

Barack Obama's judgment and his leadership ability. (We must admit, however, that John McCain's choice of Sarah Palin was equally questionable, even though she was actually more experienced than Barack Obama at that time.) As always, whenever VP Biden does or says something ridiculous, the standard answer is, "Oh, that's just Joe. He had good intentions." What nonsense.

The best of intentions can lead to big mistakes, like Solyndra, Fast and Furious and so many more. But even a big mistake can be an opportunity for a big recovery—to fix it. This is a parallel to the point about failures. You can learn from failures if they aren't fatal—and if you take the right kind of corrective actions. You can learn from mistakes too, if they aren't too serious—and if you don't deny or ignore them. But if you repeat your mistakes over and over, no matter how good your intentions, you fit the "description of insanity" and you prove that you haven't learned from your failures.

To do things the right way, you must make decisions based on the best facts and most likely expected outcomes, preferably over which you and the people involved, can have some element of control; not just because they sounded nice or looked good. You must always do your "due diligence," because as we discussed earlier in the chapter about "making up answers," you will have to answer for your decisions. Given his list of mistakes, missteps and outright failures, Barack Obama should also have to answer— when it comes to election time in 2012. He has already defined what should happen, when he said to Bob Schieffer (about the economy) on CBS Face the Nation in 2009, "...If I don't have this done in three years, then there's going to be a one-term proposition." So be it.

OBAMA PRESIDENCY BACKGROUND AND TYPICAL ISSUES

Throw money at problems to speed up the results. Right? No! Wrong. Case in point: Stimulus #1—nothing much happened because the money was used wrong. Case in point #2: QE2—nothing much happened because it was a misguided attempt to speed up the cycle with "fertilizer." Coming attractions: The Obama Job Bill: Probable outcome? DOA—It will never get out of Congress because it makes the same old mistakes. Remember the definition of insanity—"doing the same things over and over and expecting different outcomes"? Misspent giveaways, patronage, pork, "shovel-ready" jobs that weren't "shovel-ready" at all and throwing money at the economy doesn't fix anything. It just leaves America and Americans "another day older and deeper in debt. Good intentions are simply not good enough when they lead to consistently bad outcomes.

∾

"A liberal is someone who feels a great debt to his fellow man, which debt he proposes to pay off with your money."

—G. Gordon Liddy

∾

CHAPTER EIGHTEEN

IF SOMETHING IS TOO BIG TO FAIL, IT WILL!

How do you eat an elephant? One bite at a time. If you create things that are so big and massive that virtually no one can control them, then you—and they—are destined to fail. What happens if you choose to dance with an elephant? The elephant will want to lead! "Doubling down" on a failed endeavor just to "save face" (by not admitting you were wrong) creates even larger problems than the original mistake. If you make something bigger still, and it's not necessarily better, (think of the big Wall Street banks or government entities like Fannie Mae and Freddie Mac) then when it fails, it will make an even bigger mess. The old boxing adage comes to mind: "The bigger they are, the harder they fall."

Another way to think of this is it's far better to break down big projects into a series of smaller, more manageable pieces, and complete each of them successfully. It is like building a wall of bricks. Each brick is not such a big deal, but lay enough of them straight and true, on a sound foundation, and you have a sturdy wall. You can't "build a wall" all at once.

If you have ever heard a great investor speak, they will often say, "Be quick to cut your losses and ride your winners." It is the same thing with leading organizations. If you know something is not working, don't keep trying to make it work, wasting time and resources. Remember the definition of insanity: "Doing the same thing over and over again and expecting a different result." So many organizations and leaders want something to work so badly that they keep throwing good money after bad to keep it propped up, until it finally comes crashing down.

President Obama has done this not only with Solyndra-type investments, but also with Freddie Mac and Fannie Mae, the US economy, Obamacare, and host of other "too big to fail" (but still do fail) programs. To be fair, he is not the only leader who has made this kind of mistake. If you look at Europe, especially the Greek situation, it is a somewhat similar example. Greece is totally bankrupt from spending so much more than it takes in, that it has almost collapsed the Euro. What is the answer—to keep bailing out the failures, over and over? No way! That is just "kicking the can down the road" and the problem does not go away. Next in line for bailouts are which countries? Italy, Spain, Ireland and Portugal are all afflicted with similar problems to Greece. What happens when they start failing? This is the model President Obama is emulating

The European Community is so committed to its policies surrounding the Euro, that it does not want to admit that Greece, (and the others?) have failed. In the U.S., it is the same with Social Security and Medicare, the entitlements that form the so-called "3rd rail of politics." These programs combined have a projected deficit of over $50 trillion dollars. That requires more bailout money than exists anywhere.

At some point neither Europe, nor the U.S., nor China, nor anyone else, will be able to "kick that can down the road." These issues—runaway spending, enormous deficits and lack of fiscal irresponsibility—will have to be faced and dealt with. It will be painful and take a lot of courage from those in charge to speak the truth and to figure out what to do. But the alternative to the pain of fixing the problem is total collapse.

Always remember the phrase "cut your losses and ride your winners." You will have much more success in stopping things before they get "too big to fail" and come crashing down. Another way to put it is in the sound business adage: "When you are in something, if you knew then what you know now you wouldn't get into it, then find a way to get out of it." Fast! Seems like a good lesson to take away from this chapter.

OBAMA PRESIDENCY BACKGROUND AND TYPICAL ISSUES

The too big, too complex and too risky list is too long: GSE's[9] like Fannie Mae & Freddie Mac, the US Postal Service, entitlements like Social Security, Medicare/Medicaid, and massive new legislation like Obamacare, (plus the six largest "too big to fail" banks in the USA holding more than 60% of all assets in America)—and that is just a partial list. This demands a president and an administration that operates on more than academic theories and political expediency. Even if it isn't Barack Obama's fault per se—but many feel that it is—he stepped up to a job and task that he was not prepared to handle.

Ꮼ

"If you think health care is expensive now, wait until you see what it costs when it's free!"

—P. J. O'Rourke

Ꮼ

---

9   GSE: Government Sponsored Entities—which are neither public nor private but part way in between, and are still supported with substantial governmental funding to cover their losses.

CHAPTER NINETEEN

THROWING MONEY AT PROBLEMS DOESN'T FIX THEM

One of the most common mistakes made by inexperienced managers and executives is to "throw money at problems" with the expectation that the problems will go away. They don't. In fact, they often get worse. In this respect, some problems are like the Sci-Fi monsters that absorb energy from weapons used to attack them and then grow even stronger.

Feed a problem with a lot of ill-advised spending and the problem often grows larger and more difficult to solve. Make no mistake; there are times when a shortage of money or lack of funding IS the problem. Businesses encounter that all the time when they run out of working capital and get in a cash flow bind. At other times, there is a desperate need for the funding to develop and/or implement a "game changing idea." But these instances are no excuse for "throwing money at every problem."

There are instances like Stimulus 1, where the huge amount of money (Over $800 billion!) is now considered by many Keynesian economists to have been too little! In fact, the amount of money "thrown at the problem" was not the biggest issue. It was how that money was misused, misspent or wasted.

There are some instances where Federal stimulus programs can do real economic good—such as infrastructure repair and rebuilding. Unfortunately, far too few of these were found or funded in Stimulus 1. The Obama administration made a common error, which is symptomatic of inexperience. They solved the "apparent problems"—which makes them temporarily look and feel good (politically)—but they don't solve the "root causes" of the problems.

There are only three steps required to solve any problem and the steps are fairly straightforward:
1. Understand the problem
2. Define the problem
3. Solve the problem

The mistakes this president and his administration keeps making is jumping to step 3 without adequately completing steps 1 and 2. The job creation challenge is a good example. The jobs problem is symptomatic of a weak economic environment and structural changes in the global economy. Following the financial crisis, companies cut back in every possible way to save money and are now holding onto that cash. Banks were damaged by the financial crisis, so even when they now have money to lend, they are very wary of the risks in lending it. Job creation is not the solution directly; jobs are the outcome of a solution to the real problem—weak economic growth. The real problem is weakness in the economy.

Enter a president who is arguably the most anti-business occupant of the White House in a long time. Businesses close ranks and stop investing in anything with much risk. Of course President Obama talks a good game about not being anti-business, but his actions speak so much more loudly than his words that he might as well not speak about it. He can pal around with Jeffrey Immelt all he wants, but as long as there continues to be an avalanche of new laws such as Dodd-Frank and Obamacare, rampant uncertainty (A 2-month payroll tax extension? Really?), and oppressive new regulations by Obama's minions in the EPA, NLRB, CPSC, HHS, TSA, etc., etc., Obama's administration proves over and over that he and they are de-facto anti-business.

Businesses feel negative, oppressed, uncertain and concerned; they lack the confidence to invest. Businesses that would like to invest and grow again are afraid of what the government will do next. Huge amounts of corporate earnings are trapped overseas, and cannot be repatriated without incurring a huge tax hit, so there they stay, to be invested outside the USA, or just sit on multinational corporate balance sheets, unproductive. These problems cascade down to impact tens of millions of consumers (many of them unemployed or underemployed) who are frightened and uncertain about their future, and doubtful that it will get better any time soon.

Fear, uncertainty and doubt are paralyzing the United States, and this has similarly paralyzed business growth. That is what is impeding job growth in the USA. Fix that problem, and the jobs problem will get fixed along with it.

Only private sector growth creates lasting jobs, which create wealth, which in turn generates more tax revenue. It doesn't work the other way around. Every government job created by "throwing money at the problem" is funded on the backs of taxpayers, and squeezes out private sector investments.

That is what is meant by "understanding the problem" and "defining the problem." Solving the problem is not simple, but it starts with getting the government "off the back" of the private sector, and encouraging investment by removing the penalties, and enhancing the likelihood that investors will be able to realize good returns by taking risks with their money.

When leaders (in business or in government) do not understand these problems, they cannot define them clearly and then they define them wrong, they solve the wrong problem—and fail. That's what is happening in America right now

Example 1—Cash for Clunkers: "Throwing good money after bad," didn't really work in "Cash for Clunkers"). Analysis by auto experts at Edmunds.com concluded that of the 690,000 vehicles sold, only about 125,000 of them were vehicles that would not have been sold anyway. The other sales were just "pulled forward" from normally expected purchases. Thus taxpayers really ended up paying an extra $24,000 per incremental car sold to "create new demand." Not a very good deal is it?

If you throw enough money at something you can waste a lot of money, because funding a bad idea or the wrong plan won't improve it—it just takes the resources away from good ideas and right plans. (See prior chapter "the bigger they are, the harder they fall," and the bigger mess they make.)

Example 2—Stimulus I: The post mortem on Stimulus 1 was that each job cost either $278,000 per job created or (after using inflated job creation numbers that no one could substantiate) $185,000 per job created. Both of these are much higher than the initial, (still ridiculous) figure of "only" $72,400 per job created— which was a bad investment even at that.

What kind of game are the government and the president playing? "Throw money at the problems?" Take $72,400 of taxpayers' money and spend it to create a job that pays, maybe, $50,000 per year. Does that sound like a good deal? Nope! But as pointed out earlier, throwing money at problems actually makes them worse.

The real cost per job was (either) $278,000—4 times the initial estimate, (or) $185,000—almost 3 times the initial estimate— depending on which "post mortem" analysis you believe. Did throwing money at this jobs problem solve anything? Nope! It did waste a lot of money, and nobody is quite sure where it all went. But everyone agrees that too few jobs resulted, and they cost too much per job to "create."

We feel it is important to point out a simple fact here that, amazingly most politicians will never acknowledge. We hear our politicians speak all the time about how "we need to create jobs." Well, the simple fact of the matter is that government truly cannot create a job. It can only make it easier or harder for those in the private sector to do so. Government's only source of money is in levies on the earnings and wealth of its citizens.

As alluded to earlier, any "government job" that is created just happens by taking the money to pay for it out of the hands of taxpayers in the private sector. The government does not and cannot create wealth; it can only "take it" (or redistribute it). Since about two-thirds of the U.S. economy depends on consumer spending, it is no wonder Obama's policies have failed to work. This president and his administration are applying solutions to a completely different (perceived) problem than allowing business and the private sector to have what it needs to drive the economy—certainty—so it can invest without worrying how the government will try to change the rules and deny them their rightful returns on those investments.

As a leader you must always remember to first understand any problem and its root issues before looking at a solution or spending more money on it. Many times these things happen because of emotional attachment to a project or initiative. Remember to stay logical, avoid personal bias, and look at any problem from all points of view before moving toward a solution. Understand, define and then solve the problem—in that order.

OBAMA PRESIDENCY BACKGROUND AND TYPICAL ISSUES

Biggest example—To reiterate: Stimulus 1 cost $278,000 (or $185,0000) per job created (or saved) and unemployment is "reduced to 9%?" Is spending taxpayers' money at $24,000 per car to sell and additional 125,000 cars a good idea? Perhaps some jobs were created, but since many of the cars sold were foreign makes, many jobs were not US jobs. Was using the government to "bail out GM and Chrysler" and force bankruptcy restructuring a good way to spend $24 billion of taxpayers' money, when a normal Chapter 11 bankruptcy would have had the same effect—and be done legally?

Then the government illegally took huge amounts of money (bond value) away from legal bondholders and "gave" a much bigger share of GM to the UAW, President Obama's big supporter. (That case is currently making its way through the courts, and when decided, could cost the government billions more.)

ᢙ

"I contend that for a nation to try to tax itself into prosperity is like a man standing in a bucket and trying to lift himself up by the handle."

—Winston Churchill

ᢙ

CHAPTER TWENTY

ALL SPENDING IS NOT AN "INVESTMENT"

Investments have a measurable return. Thus, spending is not the same as investment—unless the return can be identified and quantified. "A rose by any other name, may not smell as sweet," but a lousy investment always stinks—no matter what words are used to describe it.

As we discussed earlier, "Words and how you use them are powerful." There is no better example than when President Obama changed his wording from "spending" to "investment." The American people have caught on to how much spending has been taking place and have had enough of it. Thus, now President Obama has changed his words and emphasizes that we must start "investing." Well, as we know his track record of investing is not very good and the last thing people want is more, ill-advised spending...or we mean... investments—which provide little or no return and lots of debt.

True investments have a quantifiable return that can be measured to decide if the investment is good or bad, a success or failure. There is accountability associated with this approach. Blindly spending and throwing money at something to look good (look as if you are "fixing something" that way) does not.

Organizations and leaders have these same problems in business settings. Many times decisions are made, and money is spent without thinking through what the return should or will be and when it will occur. The people in charge, "just want to do something!" Doing something for the sake of doing something is almost always a bad idea that backfires. It is usually done based on emotional and not logical thought, frequently intended to make an organization, group or leader look better superficially.

Internet grocery pioneer Webvan illustrated the error in thinking that throwing money at something was an "investment." It committed to an extensive warehousing and distribution network without first developing enough customers and revenue to support it. The obvious result followed—it ran out of money, had way too much overhead, and rather quickly went into bankruptcy—spending does not equal investment unless there is a measurable, and adequate return on the money.

The online video streaming company Netflix is an example of this lesson (turned inside out). In mid-2011 Netflix stock was at an all-time high. The company was growing at an incredible rate, adding subscribers and starting to move into foreign markets. It looked as though Netflix would be the next darling of Wall Street. But in just a few short months, Netflix stock plummeted over 70%!

Why? It was all due to one unexplainable economic (investment idea?) decision—instead of spending more money, it would try to collect more money, without actually delivering any more value to its customers. The company abandoned the model that had brought it so much success, and split its services, so it could charge its subscribers more money for essentially the same product. It even decided to spin off part of the business into a separate company, in hopes of disguising the intent of this move, which was to raise prices, and create an "apparently greater value" for prospective investors.

Well, you most likely know the result. Customers left Netflix in droves, the spinoff being created, died before it ever got off the ground, and the company is still digging out of a self-imposed quagmire. Netflix' new "investment idea" turned out to cost its loyal customers more money and greatly damaged its reputation, destroying billions in potential stock value (of prospective future investors) in the process.

As a leader you must carefully think through the motives behind your investments and what the probable ramifications of these moves might be. You must also be very conscious of, and be able to quantify what the real returns on investment will be. You cannot gamble and decide just to "do something to make it look like you are doing something." The fact is that all spending is not investment; sometimes it is just senseless or misguided spending, with little hope of an adequate return.

OBAMA PRESIDENCY BACKGROUND AND TYPICAL ISSUES

When the president talks about "investment" on still more welfare-related projects or on green/alternative energy projects, or to improve education, he is much more likely talking about "spending"—since the return on any of those is, thus far, only theoretical and might be simply an illusion. Words do make a difference. The $500 million "loan guarantee" to Solyndra[10] was lost because "it sure looked good," before it failed rapidly and dramatically, costing American taxpayers. There are too many others like this one to even list them all here—but billions of taxpayer dollars are "invested" in risky concepts. Most of these were admittedly known to be "gambles!" Whether these and other of Obama's other "pet projects" are truly "investments" or just more "spending," cannot yet be determined, since too few of them have shown positive returns thus far.

---

10   PricewaterhouseCoopers LLP warned Solyndra had financial troubles deep enough to "raise substantial doubt about its ability to continue as a going concern" in an audit released in March 2010. Two months later, President Barack Obama visited its Fremont plant and told workers the factory shows "the promise of clean energy isn't just an article of faith." http://www.bloomberg.com/news/2011-09-13/solyndra-failure-is-seen-blunting-obama-drive-to-aid-clean-energy-startups.html

෬ඁ

"A government which robs Peter to pay Paul can always depend on the support of Paul."

—George Bernard Shaw

෬ඁ

CHAPTER TWENTY-ONE

VICTORY BY DEFINITION ISN'T VICTORY

What constitutes a victory? Most would say that it is the attainment of a goal or triumph over a competitor. In politics, victory means something different. It means whatever someone wants it to mean, to make them look good. Far too often a politician will put out an objective and when the objective fails to be achieved, they change the definition of the objective to make the outcome look like some type of "win."

Barack Obama and his administration have used this approach frequently. Whether it is their prediction of "creating"—later changed to "creating or saving"—jobs, investment "gambles" like Solyndra, or stimulus programs that don't stimulate much of anything except the deficit, there is no shortage of examples of claiming victory by re-definition.

After policy blunders that have strained relations with Israel, another of his mistakes in this area was in Egypt with support for the removal of Mubarak. The mistake was not that removing Mubarak, a decades long dictator, was the wrong choice, but the fact that the Obama administration constantly defended those removing him from power. (We could have changed the names and made this paragraph about Libya and Qaddafi.) The biggest concern now is that the group—the Muslim Brotherhood—that will control the rebels that ousted Mubarak will in turn implement their dangerous beliefs and policies in Egypt. (Ditto: Libya. Who's really in charge?)

The Obama administration constantly defended the rebel group saying it was not the Muslim Brotherhood and would not implement the dangerous practices that everyone (especially Israel) feared. The brotherhood has all but said they (along with Iran) want to eradicate Israel from the face of the earth.

So what happened? Not long after Mubarak was ousted, the beliefs and policies that everyone feared began to be put in place. Christians were persecuted and fighting erupted, which continues. The Muslim brotherhood has gained strength in the government, and it is implementing the same dangerous policies that the Obama administration said would never come to pass.

So what does the administration do? They "move the goal posts" and change their narrative, redefining what its support was all about, and what "victory" really meant. Examples like this represent politics at its worst and the Obama presidency uses it often. "Victories" like this, no matter how they are "redefined," are really mislabeled failures.

As a leader, team member, or contributor, you must always clearly define success. What outcome or victory are you seeking? Cheating or "moving the goal line" doesn't really win the game; it just gives the illusion of victory. You must not redefine goals to make it seem like a victory was achieved when it wasn't, just to show a better outcome. Redefining goals to make it appear as if they were reached is both denial and intellectual dishonesty. Cheaters always get caught—eventually.

In the competitive politics of corporate life this kind of attractive trap is commonly used to create the illusion of victory (by definition). Often this can be done by only presenting part of the facts, or distorting the apparent results by mathematical manipulation. But, as you may have heard, "figures don't lie, but liars figure," and hope not to get caught.

Leaders must get everyone aligned with a crystal clear definition of victory, which then makes it much easier to achieve. This is a benefit for everyone involved, whatever their roles. It is when conflicting messages are repeatedly sent that it becomes harder to stay aligned and achieve victory. Define success and then go after it and achieve it. Don't try to claim victory by redefining failure into success—that just makes the failure worse—and more obvious.

OBAMA PRESIDENCY BACKGROUND AND TYPICAL ISSUES

The debacle about what was a job "created" and what was a job "saved" was the most blatant attempt to redefine a failure—Stimulus 1, a rich source of multiple failures—into a success. It fooled no one and made the perpetrators of it look like manipulators. The same approach is now being attempted over and over—first in the debt ceiling confrontation, and more recently in failed negotiations of the Super Committee. Worse yet, the savings claimed by sequestration are little more than deceptive illusions, enabled by government's contrived baseline-budget bookkeeping. The claimed savings are only a reduction from how much the spending would have increased if nothing were done—that means there were/are no real savings at all—just more and more spending.

∞

"In my many years I have come to a conclusion that one useless man is a shame, two is a law firm and three or more is a Congress."

—John Adams

∞

V
HOPE IS NOT A STRATEGY

"People love change; they just don't like transition."

—Matthew Kelly

CHAPTER TWENTY-TWO

CHANGE FOR CHANGE SAKE CAN BE HARMFUL

Never underestimate the difficulty of change. Change is not easy. Don't misunderstand change for progress; they are two different things entirely. When considering the need to change, always think about the answers to these four questions:

- Why change?
- Why now?
- Why me/us?
- What next?

Far too often, change is used as a way to hide or avoid nagging problems that will continue to impact an organization whether changes are made or not. "Change" sounds good though: "We're making some changes, and everything will be better." But will it?

In today's fast paced society, people are quick to jump to change as the solution when in fact, most times it has as great a chance of making things worse, as making them better. The 4 questions above will help you to consider and to better understand, if change is really necessary. The questions help you consider what the change actually involves, and what impact it could have.

When Barack Obama campaigned, his slogan was "Hope and Change." But change to what? Obama never clearly defined the changes he was going to make. He spoke repeatedly about many kinds of change, most of which he has not accomplished. He also made grand promises, most of which he has not kept. Even in instances where he did name specific changes, he has largely been either unwilling—or unable—to implement many of them. (E.g., Eliminating earmarks and closing Guantanamo, to name just two.)

Barack Obama used words powerfully to sound good, but actually said very little about what he'd really change—and less about how he'd do that. It's easy to make grand sounding plans. The tough part is making the change work. Every once in a while Obama would let something slip out, such as that he wanted to "fundamentally change America," (We see that now—how's that going?) or "spread the wealth around" (For which "Joe the Plumber " called him out.) But for the most part he carefully avoided defining the changes—it was just, "I'll do something different than George W. Bush," and even that proved a hard promise to keep in many areas. Now that President Obama has been in office for 3 years, the American people have learned more and more what he meant by change, and for the most part, they do not like it.

"Change," meant increasing the size, reach and cost of government. Consider how Obama crammed through his health-care bill. He was all over the country, constantly on TV, making statements about "the country not being what it once was," talking about spending being out of control while giving billions to companies going bankrupt, and attacking/demonizing groups of US citizens (or in Las Vegas' case, whole cities). The change Obama had in mind was not in step with or in the best interest of many Americans. Barack Obama behaved far differently once he was governing than when he was campaigning—and his policies—and politics differed too. People notice things like that.

"Change for change sake" is the wrong reason to do something. What if the change makes things worse? What if it is the wrong change? Is America better off for the changes Barack Obama's presidency has made? Many do not think so. The records say that

America is not better off for the changes during the first three years of Barack Obama's presidency:

1. Record number of Americans unemployed & underemployed.
2. Record length of time Americans have remained unemployed.
3. Record highest Federal government spending in history.
4. Record highest Federal budgets in history.
5. Record highest Federal budget deficits ever.
6. Record highest projected 10-year future Federal deficits.
7. Record number of governmental regulations added.
8. Record number of pages in bills signed into law.
9. Record number of TV appearances justifying one of them (Obamacare).
10. Record number of TV appearances of any president in history.
11. Record number of times the word "I" was used in presidential speeches.
12. Record (low) number of times attending church while president.
13. Record amount of Teleprompter use by any president in history.
14. Record amount of money spent on an election campaign.
15. Record amount of money planned to be spent on a re-election campaign.

These are not records to be proud of, nor are these changes desirable to most Americans. Real, positive change comes from thoughtful, strategically planned decisions leading to carefully considered outcomes.

As a leader (or contributor), you must understand that change is not easy and can either make things better (if done well) or worse (if done poorly). With that in mind, decisions to change should not be made too quickly, or without due diligence, and only with a well-defined plan to make the change into a reality.

This does not mean that you need overanalyze, or spend countless hours of "analysis paralysis." It does mean that if you are going to make changes, that you must very carefully answer the 4 questions at the start of this chapter, and be crystal clear on what your objectives are and how you will achieve them.

The risk of disruption due to change is also compounded by the number of "news" involved in the change. One "new" thing is hard to change; two "news" is four times as hard; three is nine times as hard, and so forth. No one has yet counted the number of "news" in Obamacare—but there are far too many in just one bill.

Perhaps it is good to close this chapter with a quote that is 500 years old, and is as true today as it was then. This statement proves that the difficulty of change has been recognized and appreciated for centuries, and that "change for change sake" is often a very dangerous course of action.

"We must bear in mind, then, that there is nothing more difficult and dangerous, or more doubtful of success, than an attempt to introduce a new order of things in any state. For the innovator has for enemies all those who derived advantages from the old order of things, whilst those who expect to be benefited by the new institutions will be but lukewarm defenders. This indifference arises in part from fear of their adversaries who were favoured by the existing laws, and partly from the incredulity of men who have no faith in anything new that is not the result of well-established experience. Hence it is that, whenever the opponents of the new order of things have the opportunity to attack it, they will do it with the zeal of partisans, whilst the others defend it but feebly, so that it is dangerous to rely upon the latter."
—*Niccolo Machiavelli (1469-1527)*

OBAMA PRESIDENCY BACKGROUND AND TYPICAL ISSUES

Some of the new EPA & CPSC regulations were promulgated not because there was a clearly defined benefit (or danger) but because there was technology that could now achieve tighter standards—with little or no consideration of the cost and unintended consequences. The new NLRB rulings, including the controversial Boeing/South Carolina ruling, and shortened lead time to union elections, were born of the frustration by Democratic union supporters at being unable to pass the Employee Free Choice Act ("Card-check Bill"), which they thought Obama would help them do. They felt the need to regulate what they couldn't legislate—and/or make changes for change sake—to look like they were "doing something."

☙

"The inherent vice of capitalism is the unequal sharing of the blessings. The inherent blessing of socialism is the equal sharing of misery."

—Winston Churchill

☙

CHAPTER TWENTY-THREE

WISHING DOESN'T MAKE IT HAPPEN

Good ideas are "a dime a dozen." Something might be a "good idea," but this only matters if someone takes action on it and it actually works. Wishing might be a good idea…until it clashes with reality. Pipe dreams are just that, dreams. The key is to know how to turn good ideas into action and positive results, to achieve defined goals and outcomes.

In order for something to cease being a dream or a wish, it takes strong action and effort to make it a reality. Many politicians use the tactic of stating a grand dream of what something can be, wishing perhaps, to get people emotionally involved, in order to get elected. It is amazing how quickly that dream fades once they are in office; often it is never mentioned again, unless by an opponent in the next election.

This may be where Barack Obama has had some of his most visible failures as a President. "This was the moment when the rise of the oceans began to slow and our planet began to heal," he said. This phrase is among his most grandiose pronouncements. He may have "hoped" that would happen. Or it may have simply been a compelling turn of a phrase. As a candidate, Barack Obama's soaring rhetoric painted a grandiose dream that he would bring everyone together, that the nation would no longer be divided, and that all would come together under his leadership.

Sadly, the exact opposite has happened. Under Obama, the U.S. is more divided than ever and Obama's leadership is at the heart of the divisiveness. Whether it is using class warfare tactics with groups, or to say, "I won the election and this is how it will be," to his Republican counterparts, his scolding speeches, or his many other similar actions, Obama has been a divider, not a uniter. Even more important is the fact that, as mentioned earlier, he has taken few effective actions to bring the country together. He doesn't know how.

Contrast Obama's failures with Ronald Reagan's success, when he spoke to Americans about a dream of America being a "shining city on a hill," and then acted decisively to make that dream a reality. Under Reagan, the U.S. had the largest peacetime expansion in history. Why? Because Reagan's beliefs and the policies behind them, made it happen. He acted every day on the goal of making his dream a reality.

As a leader, when you state a vision or goal, you must not only allow others that are involved to have input, and be a part of it, but you must also take the responsibly for showing everyone involved a clear set of actions to make that dream a reality...otherwise, it remains just a dream. People will get excited for a short while, but without a clear plan of action, they will quickly lose interest and the dream and the vision will fade.

Since John has written many times before about the role of a leader, and it seems appropriate to share it here.

The role of a leader is:

- To create a clear understanding of the current reality, and
- A healthy dissatisfaction with it (the current situation);
- To help develop a shared vision of a more desirable future situation;
- To create the belief that there is a viable path from the former to the latter;
- To create an environment in which people are motivated to embark on the journey to that future.

Then a leader must assume certain responsibilities:
The responsibilities of a leader are:

- To help the organization remove or overcome obstacles on the journey;
- To assure that the resources needed for the journey are available or can be obtained.
- To provide encouragement, honest feedback (positive or negative) and continued support during the journey.
- To take part in the journey.

It is in fulfilling these responsibilities that the Obama presidency has failed so badly. The president and his staff have simply been unable to translate their grand visions into execution. This is a failing of leadership in the extreme. The leader must first fulfill his/her role and then be willing to accept the corresponding responsibilities—to focus on execution with those involved. Then, and only then, can the dream and the vision become a reality.

OBAMA PRESIDENCY BACKGROUND AND TYPICAL ISSUES

Green energy investments were made without adequate verification of the fiscal or technological soundness of the choices: e.g., failed gambles on Solyndra-type investments... and many others. Threats and penalties to accelerate stopping the Gulf oil leak any sooner were hollow and not actionable due to uncertain remediation methods for the oil that contaminated the Gulf and delaying permission for states like Louisiana to place physical barriers to protect their wetlands made the damage worse. Denying Americans the benefit of its huge oil/gas reserves whether in ANWR, North Dakota, West Virginia or via the Keystone Pipeline, are all symptoms of a person who believes in his dream of sustainable energy sources—but has no idea how to make it into a reality—so he simply impedes others from pursuing their actionable plans.

∽

Three frogs were sitting on a log. One decided to jump into the pond. How many were left? Did you answer two? Think again. I didn't say one jumped in; I just said one DECIDED to jump in. There's a big difference between deciding to do something and actually doing it.

CHAPTER TWENTY-FOUR

TACTICAL EXECUTIVES LOSE... STRATEGIC EXECUTIVES WIN

What is the difference between a strategist and a tactician? It is important to first define the difference between a strategy and a tactic. A tactic is used to execute strategy, or to attain a quick or short-term gain, en route to the goals of the strategy. Tactical executives seem to get a lot of things done, but somehow never get where they need to go. They can't execute effectively if they have no plan—which is the heart of a strategy. A tactic is an important part of the strategy, but alone, it is not enough to achieve any but fragmentary, piecemeal goals. This is true whether speaking about members of Congress, the President of the United States—or leaders in many other settings, public and private sector alike.

A strategy is a well-defined plan made up of multiple elements that are combined to reach an end goal. A strategic executive will always win over a tactical executive. Tactical executives think short term and make decisions on things to do now, in a piecemeal way, instead of looking at the context of the whole.

Strategic executives choose a vision of the future and work toward reaching it. The fact that US Representatives are reelected every two years, tends to lead to a great deal of tactical, short term thinking in Congress as well. The role of the leader—in this case the president of the country—is to "lead;" to integrate these tactical short term approaches into a larger, longer range strategy, and then build broad-based consensus behind that strategy.

For example, if tactical sales managers are not getting sales from team efforts, their typical response might be to push the team put in more effort. "Work it harder," "Make more calls" or "Spend more time cold-calling," you might hear them say. A strategic executive will look at the team and ask different questions:

- "Why is the team not getting it done with their current efforts?"
- "What is getting in their way?"
- "Is there something wrong with their/our approach?"
- "Where can we remove or change approaches that are not working and focus more on those that are working, etc.?"

Once the strategic executive figures things out, then s/he can actually fix the problem and not just react to bits and pieces of it like a tactical executive does. Smart strategic executives always have a backup plan—usually two or three in mind—in case the first plan doesn't work as intended.

Barack Obama has proven to be a very tactical, reactive executive—partly because he has been unsuccessful at building coalitions to do anything else. He speaks strategically in his speeches, but if you listen closely, he only talks around the issues. He hardly ever gets ahead of the problems that arise to define that broad-based strategic and tactical compromise. Thus he is always behind the problems, reacting to them.

Many times, it is because he waits to see what the "polls" and public opinion says before he acts, or where his "base" and his "opposition" will be—or want him to be. Or, at other times, Obama visions are so grand, and so far into the future (for execution) that he cannot find a way to bridge from the current reality to his far off, future aspiration. In these cases, President Obama's "grand strategies" are much easier to talk about than to convert into actionable plans to execute successfully. Remember the reference to his soaring speech about how *"the rise of the oceans began to slow and our planet began to heal?"* Alternative energy development and the jobs it will create, is just one of the most glaring examples of this.

Strategies where there is no idea how to executive them, are little more than "hopes." Perhaps this is entirely consistent with his campaign theme: "hope." It is much easier to resort to short-term tactics that play to campaign themes than to aspire to bigger strategic wins. Tacticians prefer dealing with comfortable situations where the feedback is immediate, or those where there is no feedback, and they can practice "victory by definition."

The 2011 debt ceiling debate was a good example. President Obama could have stepped in much earlier, and more proactively if he could have worked with both sides (strategically). He might have found enough common (tactical) ground that the partisan agendas could have been resolved around a core of set of principles and solutions. That would have permitted progress toward getting things done ahead of the deadline that he knew was coming for months. And yet, it was easier to wait, and "hope" things would somehow get resolved by dropping in and interjecting himself tactically, while under the pressure of a deadline. Thus failing to get results, he made yet another speech, blaming Congress.

He delayed, then abdicated and/or delegated the hard strategic work, allowing the polarization to build insurmountable walls of resistance, while he was "hoping" to step in at the very last minute to try for a tactical victory, through the power of his position. This clearly illustrates how, "Hope is not a strategy."

Operating in this manner offered Obama a "tactical excuse," by using statements like (in an interview with CBS Evening News anchor Scott Pelley on Social Security checks), "I cannot guarantee that those checks go out on August 3rd if we haven't resolved this issue. Because there may simply not be the money in the coffers to do it." Nonsense!

Anyone who understands this matter knows full well that the checks could have gone out no matter what occurred. There was ample cash flowing through the US government each week, and Obama's Treasury Secretary Timothy Geithner was in control of all the departments responsible to make this happen. Money could have been diverted from different sources and for that matter (theoretically) the Social Security money was already there, "in the (mythical) 'trust fund'." In truth, money is fungible and it has no predetermined identity until it is deposited into a given place and spent for a given purpose. For Obama to say "the checks might not go out" was the height of disingenuousness.

Barack Obama was using a "scare tactic"—an age old tactical move—in hopes of forcing public opinion to pressure an agreement within an impending deadline. This is as far from strategic leadership as imaginable, and in some views, is not really leadership at all. This fact was recognized by the leaders of Congress (of both parties) who decided to work around President Obama instead of through him—and said so. This situation provides an excellent example of how tactical executives trap themselves, and get into trouble.

This "gridlock" of Congress and lack of early and consistent (strategic) Presidential leadership was worsened by how President Obama alienated Republican Congressional leaders (and even some of his Democratic base) through his disdain and open criticism. The result: the US lost one of its Triple A credit ratings. To be fair, the intractability of Congress clearly shares the blame for this outcome with the president. The American public knows this and rightfully disrespects both parts of government for failing them.

However, America has historically looked to the president and his White House staff to work with Congressional leaders strategically, and well ahead of such crises, to make sure they need not be resolved by last minute, tactical maneuvers. When Harry Truman was President he viewed the responsibility for many things as depicted in his desk sign: "The buck stops here." With Barack Obama, the sign might as well say, "The blame starts here."

This entire incident should be no surprise since it has been three years since the US has had an official budget. In one of the most flagrant abdications of governmental responsibility in modern memory, both the Democratic Congress of 2008-2010 and President Barack Obama have ignored their budgetary duties. In spite of budget proposals from the current House, neither the Senate nor the president seems to care much about passing a new budget—no budget makes uncontrolled spending so much easier.

So much for leadership and strategy; just pass tactical "continuing resolutions" to keep spending at astronomical rates, and "kick the deficit can down the road" until another crisis occurs. And another one will occur, and sooner rather than later.

If find yourself in a position of leadership, you must focus on having an appropriate blend of strategy and execution (tactics) among your management skills. You must thoroughly think through, well-defined, and disciplined strategies, and then translate those into the tactics to execute them, thus achieving the desired goals. Always make sure to be thinking months, or even years ahead (depending on the time frames in your environment). What will you need to be doing, how far in advance? What decisions and directions must be defined and executed now, to be ready for the future needs? Unmanaged deadlines are the enemy of strategic leaders, and the bane of tactical leaders.

Also, keep in mind to avoid just "reacting" to situations with "knee-jerk" responses. Consider the larger picture, evaluate all options to get the critical needs accomplished, and always be questioning if past or current methods are appropriate to deal with future needs and problems. Remember: "Failing to plan is the same as planning to fail." Strategic executives anticipate, evaluate, plan and act; tactical ones react, and react, and react.

OBAMA PRESIDENCY BACKGROUND AND TYPICAL ISSUES

There is a strategic flaw in thinking that the government can "create jobs." It cannot; except by hiring people to work for the government, or its surrogates. This is like a tactician bribing the operator of the scoreboard at a ball game. The score will temporarily look better, but the gains will be illusory. Only strategically planned economic growth will create jobs based on demand, which will motivate new capital spending, and then come more jobs. However, only more business friendly, less punitive government policies will truly stimulate investment, growth and demand, which will result in job creation. A strategic executive gets this; a tactical one doesn't. Artificially creating government jobs, funded by taxpayers, which do not (or should not) endure, is like bribing the scoreboard operator to win a game. Short-term fixes are just that —short term in effect—and without a longer-term strategy, they are like putting Band-Aids® on a gaping wound.

∽

"No man's life, liberty, or property is safe while the legislature is in session."

—Mark Twain (1866)

∽

CHAPTER TWENTY-FIVE

THE HUMPTY-DUMPTY PRINCIPLE

The people who break something usually are not the ones who can fix it. Einstein warned us, "We can't solve problems by using the same kind of thinking we used when we created them."[11] Even if you could "put Humpty Dumpty together again," times and circumstances would have changed enough that it still wouldn't be right.

Given those premises, it is easy to see why a popular definition of insanity is "doing the same thing over and over again and expecting a different result." The problem with many leaders is they get so comfortable with a certain process, tactic, or idea that has worked in the past that they think it can be applied to everything in the future. The problem is that the future is different from the past, either a little bit or a lot. Is it any wonder that a solution that worked in the past may not be right for the future?

And yet, many people, including this president and his staff feel compelled to use the proven wrong solutions over and over. Some people say, "You learn from experience." The only way

---

11   Albert Einstein

you learn from experience is if you stop and honestly reflect—especially when something that you thought would work, didn't work—and consider why. This is one of those times where practicing "victory by definition" is deadly. It keeps you in denial; it prevents you from learning from your failures.

These are the reasons why the Humpty Dumpty Principle holds so true. How can you believe that the people (and the practices or policies) that got you into the mess will get you out of it? If they were smart enough to get you out it, they would have kept you out in the first place, wouldn't they?

That is also why as organizations begin to fail consistently over time, the first thing that is done is to replace the leader. All too often, the outgoing leader has been blinded by mistaken perceptions of what led to success. Thus they are averse to changing how they do things.

You see this many times when something is not working. The response is "that can't be wrong, let's double down" on the efforts. In fact, throughout the Obama administration, his excuses have been that "the theory is sound, it just hasn't worked (yet) on a big enough scale," or "I guess I didn't explain it clearly enough, or the people would see how I am right," even though the policy, initiative and actions were not working.

The people could see this—when 9% measured unemployment is really more like 10-12% real unemployment, plus another 5-6% underemployment—something is clearly broken. Humpty Dumpty was clearly broken—badly.

The Obama administration's first stimulus plan (Stimulus 1) spent almost a TRILLION dollars and barely moved the economic needle. True, it added incrementally to the anemic growth in GDP, but that increase in GDP growth was unsustainable—a one-time event. The unemployment rate went up to 10%, and remained at or near 9% for well over two years, (after the administration promised it would drop below 8% due to the stimulus). What were the administration's responses? "If we hadn't done it, unemployment might have gone even higher" (an excuse and victory by definition) and "we should have made the stimulus bigger" (an excuse—throwing money at problems).

In fact, President Obama was recently campaigning to spend another HALF a TRILLION more to "help" the economy by "creating jobs." That would be in addition to the quarter billion dollar cost of further extending unemployment (again) and a continuation of the payroll tax "holiday" which was also unfunded. Has it never occurred to him that his ideas may be wrong in the first place? It was inconceivable to him that the first stimulus was not executed properly. And yet it was filled with "pork," patronage, favors and numerous other parts, only a few of which really stimulated the economy. "I guess those shovel ready projects weren't so shovel ready after all," smirked President Obama to Jeffrey Immelt in a widely televised moment of truth.

Solyndra was just the most highly publicized example of the Obama administration's mistaken beliefs. In the end Solyndra alone lost $500 million of taxpayer dollars, only to discover that the Obama administration was considering giving it still more money to prop it up. The Obama Energy Department continues to keep "investing" (spending and gambling) huge sums of taxpayer dollars in other "green energy" ventures, many of which are destined to a fate like Solyndra's.

These "green/sustainable energy initiatives" were grand ideas, if they had worked, but they didn't work, partly because of inadequate due diligence—to make sure the companies were/are viable and would use the money wisely. No one in charge had the requisite business acumen to see through these flawed investments. The first question should have been, if these companies are so good, why aren't more private sector investors clamoring to back them?

As a leader, you must realize that sometimes you have to step aside and find the right people to help you execute on initiatives. You must also realize that you do not and never will have all of the answers.... and that is ok. What you must be good at knowing is where to find the right answers and how to implement them. You must realize when what you are doing is not working, and you must find a different way, and bring in the right (different) people to do it the way it must be done to be successful. Find someone with the right expertise, to choose the right places for investments.

Do not let pride of "my way is the right way" get in the path of success. Be humble and realize that there is always somebody that may know a better solution. Take advantage of that and leverage their solutions! Einstein was right. "We can't solve problems by using the same kind of thinking we used when we created them." When Humpty Dumpty gets broken, don't even try to put him together again the same way.

OBAMA PRESIDENCY BACKGROUND AND TYPICAL ISSUES

Barack Obama has fewer people with business background in his administration than any president in modern history. Is it any wonder that his administration executes business-like initiatives poorly? Is it surprising that the Obama administration seems to be "anti-business?" No! Politicians and educators may be smart people, but no amount of theory replaces real world experience in understanding how things work in business in a free enterprise, capitalistic system.

∽

"The government is like a baby's alimentary canal, with a happy appetite at one end and no responsibility at the other."

—Ronald Reagan

∽

CHAPTER TWENTY-SIX

UNDERSTAND YOUR CUSTOMER BEFORE YOU TRY TO SELL THEM SOMETHING

In his fine book *7 Habits of Highly Effective People*, Stephen R. Covey cites as one of the habits: "Seek first to understand and then be understood." One of the first lessons professional sales people learn is to do their research. Many times, it is called "pre-call" planning. The reason this lesson is so important to professional sales people is that they realize that they must be prepared at all times and cannot afford to be caught off guard.

They seek to understand their prospect's organization, understand their prospect, learn about the industry, be conscious of the challenges that the prospect may be going through, and most importantly, make sure that they have a clear understanding of the prospect's needs and wants. What separates truly great sales people from everyone else is, as discussed in our previous chapter, that they not only have great style, but have the substance to go with it.

That means it should be no surprise that people who try to sell something to a customer (or a constituent) that they don't understand, usually fail—and miserably.   It is clear that after almost 3 years of "selling HOPE" to the American people, Barack Obama still has not done his "pre-call" planning. Again and again, time after time, he has made decisions that go against what the majority of American people believe—or want. He may have succeeded on selling them on the idea of "hope" but it was for better outcomes—not worse ones.

A business fundamental, described earlier and learned by most executives early in their careers is that there are only three steps to solving any problem, and that includes selling something to a prospective customer.

Step 1: Understand the problem (the customer)

Step 2: Define the problem (the customer's needs and wants)

Step 3: Solve the problem (for the customer)

It is surprising how many people, specifically the current occupant of the White House, attempt to solve problems that they neither understand nor have fully defined—on behalf of "customers" they neither understand nor respect—in this case, the American people.

Whether it is in health care (Obamacare), in financial regulations (Dodd-Frank), in drilling moratoriums, or in countless other regulations, President Obama has yet to listen to his customers. The irony in this is that the customers want to be heard and understood better. When that is the first step—to understand the customers needs and wants—the next step of "solving the problem" of selling them something is so much simpler.

Perhaps there was no training in Obama's community organizer, law professor or Harvard Law Review editor jobs that covered these fundamentals. Some people say that Obama doesn't listen on purpose, as he wants to do what his beliefs dictate. He either doesn't care what others think or thinks he's smarter than everyone else. That may all be so, but that behavior is certainly not going to help him curry favor when it comes re-election time. Barack Obama's core supporters, of course, share most of his beliefs and wonder why he doesn't push them even harder. Others seem to like him personally; they just don't like the results he's getting. One thing is certain. Barack Obama is getting OJT (On the Job

Training) in what is arguably the most difficult leadership position in the world. Thus he might be expected to make some mistakes.

One of our primary goals in writing this book was to spare you from suffering the pain of learning about leadership through OJT and/or mistake after mistake. If you are in a position of leadership, whether it is sales leadership or not, you are "a salesperson." In fact, you have to be a great salesperson. You must understand the multitude of "customers" (constituents) that you have (employees, superiors, partners, counterparts, etc.) and learn how to sell to each of them in their own unique, individual way. You must take the time to do your research, and your homework, and understand them—before you try to sell them on your idea, plan, or mission/vision.

If you can take the time to really figure out what your "customer" wants and then show them how working with you on the idea, plan, or mission/vision will help them to get it; they will do everything they can to help you. Zig Ziglar once said that, "You will get everything that you want if you just help others get what they want." Remember these points and apply them throughout your leadership.

OBAMA PRESIDENCY BACKGROUND AND TYPICAL ISSUES

Maybe it is unclear who are the "customers" of the president of the United States. Shouldn't it be the all of citizens (and organizations) in the USA? But this president is unclear on this, choosing instead to carve out certain groups and classes as his "customers," and cast the others into the roles of "opponents or villains." In a time when doing what is right for the country is paramount, Barack Obama often talks of doing this, but he fails to "walk his talk," assailing "greedy Wall Street Bankers," and the "millionaires ad billionaires" as classes of "customers" who should be penalized (taxed) for being too successful. Obama's underlying policy of "wealth redistribution" has been tested time and gain—"no sale!" Socialism and its various near philosophical neighbors have proven failures since the days of Karl Marx.

∾

"What this country needs are more unemployed politicians."

—Edward Langley, Artist (1928-1995)

∾

VI
TIMELESS TRUTHS

*"The truth has a million faces
but there is only one truth."*

CHAPTER TWENTY-SEVEN

TAKE CARE OF THE STAKEHOLDERS...
THEY'LL TAKE CARE OF YOU

Who are stakeholders? In a very real sense, they are your "customers," not only for what you are selling but also for what you represent. Employees/associates, customers, suppliers, shareholder/investors, and communities are all commonly considered stakeholders in a business. In a governmental unit they are simply the voters—the citizens of that governmental unit.

Not only must you know your "stakeholder customers," but also you must do everything you can to act in their best interest and take care of them to the fullest. These are also the "customers" and "investors" that an elected official must serve.

In a corporation, this means taking care of the shareholders. In a small business, it may be taking care of your small group of investors or key customers—or essential suppliers. In a non-profit, it is taking care of the donors that support it, and whoever its services benefit. As a leader within an organization, it means looking out for the best interests of those on your team. In government... this means taking care of the people who chose you, and putting their best interests and needs ahead of your own.

All stakeholders deserve the same things of their leaders: character, honesty, integrity and principles. They also expect to be communicated with honestly, and to be treated with fairness. Finally, stakeholders most of all expect to be able to trust you, and for you to be trustworthy. And that means, above all "Say (and mean) what you will do, and then do what you said you would."

As a leader, you must always be willing to put the well being and best interests of those you serve ahead of your own. Do we need to do more at this point than to ask the simple question, "Do you believe that President Barack Obama is putting your best interests ahead of his own agenda?" Despite what he says, after a look at his actual track record—what he does—the answer must be a resounding "NO."

Great leaders make sure that those they serve are always taken care of before they take care of themselves. Whether it is a great general who makes sure his troops are well fed before the officers eat, or the small business owner who skips a paycheck to make sure employees are paid on time. During tough times, a great CEO decides to forgo a bonus because the company did not perform to the standards expected of the shareholders. Great leaders will always take care of those around them and those they serve first.

Remember the phrase, "You must give up to go up." To be successful and grow as a leader, you must be willing to give up some things so that all those with a stake in the idea, plan, or mission/vision are taken care of. Never doubt the truth of this simple line: "What goes around, comes around." Sometimes it just takes a while.

OBAMA PRESIDENCY BACKGROUND AND TYPICAL ISSUES

The real question is who are the stakeholders of America? (Previously we asked who were the "customers of the president") Are America's stakeholders its citizens, the holders of its wealth, or its debtors (led by China)— or are they a much more narrowly defined ideological group that is more closely aligned with a person or a political party, and its allies? This matters a lot, and in the case of Barack Obama, it remains unclear. The answer should be, for the President of the United States of America, stakeholders are every American—first, and then our allies and friends, and finally the many foreign investors who support America—even if they do it for their own political or profit motives. And we, and our leader(s,) should act accordingly. Do we?

෮

"Democracy must be something more than two wolves and a sheep voting on what to have for dinner."

—James Bovard, Civil Libertarian (1994)

෮

CHAPTER TWENTY-EIGHT

LACK OF FOCUS WILL SINK YOU

If you're vague enough, you might think no one will notice your lack of focus, but they will. Failing to focus on the right things means that resources—time, money and talent—will be spent on the wrong things, and wasted. A lack of focus leads to wasteful complexity too. Setting priorities is one of the toughest, and most important tasks in life and in business, and in government. Focus suffers when priorities are unclear, whether yours, or those of others you work with and/or lead.

As a leader you can take on too much and hinder your effectiveness. You must be conscious not to be a "jack of all trades, but a master of none." Focus is a tough concept for some leaders, as most want to attempt more and accomplish more. The problem with this is that it causes the leader to lose focus on what are the most important tasks or duties they need to be doing to further the goal, idea, mission, vision. Any loss of focus by the leader in turn, defocuses those being led.

It's not a matter of just working hard; it's a matter of working on the right things, and not working on others. Many times when a leader has taken on too much, it will seem like they are working very hard, but they have little to show for it in actual results. This happens because their attention is distracted and focus diluted, and often placed on less important but seemingly urgent tasks. Stephen Covey has written extensively about the difference between the important and the urgent. The "urgent" demands a leader's time and attention, and consumes too much of both, keeping the leader from focusing on what's really "important."

Barack Obama, when stepping into a complex and demanding job like the presidency, was challenged to learn this, and to walk this fine line. The presidency is not an easy job in which to learn this. Early in Obama's presidency, it seemed like he was trying something new every week. He was giving a new speech about a different topic constantly, and was generally all over the place with his message. No doubt he saw all of these as topics worthy of his attention, or of importance to his political base. After all, he wanted to "fundamentally change America," and that is a very big goal on which to focus. But that is not an acceptable excuse for his lack of focus; it is simply an explanation.

His lack of focus meant there was a lot of wasted time, money, and resources. Worse yet, the choice of one set of priorities meant the exclusion of many others. Obama's intense focus on passing his health care bill meant he didn't focus on fixing the economy and the jobs issue. His argument would be that the stimulus was supposed to do that (and he probably believed that to be true), but we have learned the error of "throwing money at things" and expecting results to follow. President Obama had so many things he wanted to do while he had a Democratically controlled Congress, that he left some very important priorities until later— and that included fixing the economy.

Even if he had focused on different priorities, his ideological and policy errors would have still led to failures. Many of Obama's focus decisions came from the misguided sense that government always knows best, and he knows best of all. Thus he decided to meddle in free markets, subsidizing car sales, and forcing the auto bankruptcies and bailouts. This made it seem to Americans (and Obama himself) like he was "doing something"—and he was—it just wasn't always enough or the right thing. He took a similar approach to foreign policy, barnstorming and making speeches that were backed by far too little substance.

The minimal success of the Stimulus 1 plan to rejuvenate the economy, and the failed investments in green energy companies (Solyndra, et. al.) may both have been based on the best of intentions, but we have discussed how that is an insufficient reason to assure success. The GM bankruptcy needed to happen; it just could have happened without disenfranchising legal bondholders in favor of the UAW and spending about $25 billion of taxpayer money that was unnecessary. Meanwhile, the economy continued to languish with more Americans unemployed for longer than ever before.

Because of the many things he wanted to change, and those he needed to change, President Obama has very much been a "jack of all trades and master of none." Because of his choice of where to focus, there are fewer instances that Obama can call successes. When Obama's supporters list his "successes" the list is full of big government initiatives, bureaucratic involvement and over-reaching regulations—and a Justice Department that seems to prioritize suing American states and municipalities over keeping illicit weapons deals under control. When Americans at large list what they see during Barack Obama's three years in office, the list is full of pain—dysfunctional government, economic distress, lack of growth and joblessness.

Focus is not just about working on the right things. It is about working on them in the right way, to get the right results. The president spoke so often about what he (I, we) was doing, that the results are only now getting a chance to speak on their own merits. At times President Obama must have felt like one of those circus entertainers who sets plates spinning atop many poles and then has to run from one to the next to keep them all spinning. Eventually, he tires and plates start crashing to the ground and breaking. An example of a plate he never started spinning, one that is a presidential duty, is approving a responsible budget with fiscal/spending control.

Priority setting is the toughest job in life, in business and in government. Focus is based on what priorities are set, and in what order they are ranked. To be effective and consistently get the results you seek as a leader, you must resolve to be laser-focused on the most important things you need to do at all times. You cannot let the little things or distractions get in your way and you cannot let you yourself get off course. Even some important things must wait in line, until even more critical ones are resolved. This is a tough set of demands for any leader, especially for the president of the USA.

Many leaders are great "idea" people or "starters." Like Barack Obama, they are great at coming up with the idea and getting a group excited about it, but they quickly lose focus and are on to the next idea. The original idea never comes to fruition, or is done poorly. Great "starters," are too often terrible "finishers."

Other leaders are great "finishers," but seem to be terrible "starters." They seem to lack the creativity to come up with enough ideas, and thus are choosing from a weak list of options. The best leaders are a hybrid of both. They are the ones that choose wisely, and focus on the few great ideas and make them a reality. Great leaders are great because they come up with ideas not only from their own choices but also from the ideas of their staff—and even of their opponents. (This was one of Ronald Reagan's strengths.) Great leaders who are great finishers also rely on the knowledge, dedication and competence of their staff to get the jobs done.

They build the shared vision and focus on making sure it gets communicated and executed well. The reason these great leaders are good at both is because they set priorities thoughtfully, with considerable input. They have laser focus and clarity of purpose on getting where they planned to go and doing what they planned to do. When you think about what went into the founding of the U.S., the Revolution, and the development of the Constitution, you will no doubt see how great the founding fathers of the U.S. were in their leadership and focus of purpose.

The most important point to take away from this chapter is to always make sure you are crystal clear on where you are going, how you will get there, and who you will need to accompany you on the journey...then focus intently on what must be done to make it happen!

OBAMA PRESIDENCY BACKGROUND AND TYPICAL ISSUES

In this case, President Obama focused arguably, too much on the "wrong thing": health care, instead of focusing enough on the "right thing:" the economy. Why he did this is his personal policy choice, but it reveals a lack of understanding of balancing priorities with results. Government derives all of its revenue from the working people and companies in the country. Absent that revenue, nothing else can be funded—and that includes Obamacare. Changing the game on one-sixth of the economy, when it is crippled is like trying to run a marathon with a broken leg—a noble idea— but one that simply causes more pain, and then failure. Focus is critical; but it must be the right focus too.

ᗧ

"A government big enough to give you everything you want, is strong enough to take everything you have."

—Thomas Jefferson

ᗧ

CHAPTER TWENTY-NINE

ACCOUNTABILITY WILL MAKE YOU

O r the lack of it will break you. If you cannot be accountable, do not take on the job. Don't make promises you can't keep. Always remember, "Winners make commitments; losers make promises." Great leaders are highly accountable—for both their achievements and failures.

There are two downsides of failing to be accountable. The first it that the results expected and funded aren't delivered. It takes a tough person to stand in the midst of a failure and say, "I take responsibility for this." Excuses will hurt your ability to grow as a person and in an organization. You can only make so many excuses before people don't want to hear them from you anymore. If you want to grow as a leader and in an organization you must be known for being accountable for your actions.

The second, and more insidious problem a leader faces in the absence of being accountable is the loss of confidence in how s/he will deliver results if given the necessary resources. The result of this loss of confidence, either personal or organizational, often leads to analysis paralysis (does the Keystone pipeline come to mind?), and still more excuses followed by attempts at "victory by definition."

President Obama has become known for making excuses and changing the narrative to make failures look like successes. Saying, "I created or saved 3 million jobs," is a ridiculous statement. How do you measure a saved job? (However you want to!) You simply cannot do so with any accuracy, and that is the point. President Obama didn't want to be accountable for the fact that what he said would happen if we spent ourselves into even more debt, didn't happen. So, Obama changed the narrative—the definition of success—as an excuse for not getting the real job done. Unfortunately for him, the unemployment statistics told the story for him: instead of dropping below 8% unemployment rose to 10%.

President Obama's tenure in office, especially in his early years was filled with excuses, usually blaming others, and showing a distressing lack of accountability. For most issues, it was still "Bush's fault" or the problem was "inherited," or "…it took a long time to get in trouble, so it will take a long time to get out of it." In other cases, the American people just "didn't understand," or the Congress simply "wouldn't cooperate." This is not leadership, but a noticeable lack of it.

Accountability will make you (or not) and in Barack Obama's case, his reluctance to be accountable has exposed his failures as a leader. No matter what role you play, large or small; you are influencing or leading something or somebody. Resolve to be accountable for all aspects of your leadership, successes and failures. To turn around the earlier phrase, "Losers make promises; winners make commitments." With commitments come accountability, and with accountability comes success as a leader.

OBAMA PRESIDENCY BACKGROUND AND TYPICAL ISSUES

One of the greatest accountabilities of the president of the United States is to lead the country in domestic affairs and that includes the world's largest economy, which includes approving a responsible budget for that economy. The Obama administration's lack of private sector experience illustrates how it is unable to craft a viable economic growth strategy for the growth of USA—which is the only thing that will cause jobs to be created and investments to be made, and the staggering Federal deficit to be reined in. The majority of people in the USA will benefit economically when the US economy is growing and healthy. When government spending squeezes out private capital, it deprives the country of one of the critical elements for growth—private investment—from both here and abroad.

Barack Obama and his administration neither understand nor sub- scribe to this tenet—and thus the economy continues to suffer—failing his greatest test of accountability. If everyone is accountable, no one is account- able! In this case, "no one" happens to be the president.

৹৲

**"He that is good for making excuses is
seldom good for anything else."**

— Benjamin Franklin

৹৲

CHAPTER THIRTY

THE DEFINITION OF INSANITY

"It really should work," is a common complaint, but once again, reality sometimes "sucks." A related trap is applying old solutions to new problems. That also seldom works. We have repeatedly cited "Doing the same things over and over and expecting different results," as a common definition of insanity. Solutions must be adapted to current circumstances. Old ones are just a starting point—because those were devised to fit an entirely different time and set of circumstances. Thus, doing the same things…well, you get it.

Innovation is a key skill of great leaders. What got you there may not keep you there, is a truism for leaders. Great leaders are always innovating because they know that the landscape is in a constant state of flux, always changing, and thus they must adapt and change their strategies with it to stay successful. You see this happen in great companies that have run into trouble, realized it, and then made the changes to their business model to get themselves back on the right track.

A great example is Starbucks. When founder, Charles Shultz stepped out after almost 30 years at helm, the company started to stray off course, became stagnant, and ran into trouble, it then

had to close a number of stores and resolve several other issues—
including loss of focus. What happened?

One of the biggest things that Starbucks had done so well, for
so long, was innovating to stay ahead of competitors and imita-
tors. When Charles stepped out, some of that will to innovate was
lost. So was the focus on what made Starbucks successful—the
appeal of its aromas, its coffee and its social ambience—and everything that contributed to them. Starbucks management thought
the company could simply keep doing the "same old, same old,"
of what it had done up to that point and stay at the levels it had
achieved. They were wrong. Starbucks, in Shultz own words, "was
becoming commoditized"

After a few years out of the company, Shultz stepped back in,
bringing back his focus and innovative leadership spirit to the
company. Now Starbucks is doing incredibly well again. Its stock
value is up and the company is more popular than ever. In fact,
Charles Shultz book, _Onward: How Starbucks Fought for Its Life without Losing Its Soul,_ details how his leadership brought the company
back to success.

Schultz also gained considerable attention by announcing
that he would no longer support the current crop of political
incumbents because he was fed up with their dysfunctional leadership of our country. Since this group included Barack Obama
(where Schultz had been a big supporter), it clearly gained
the president's attention, and warranted a lengthy phone call
between Schultz and Obama. We can only hope that some of
Schultz's innovative leadership characteristics "rubbed off" on
Obama after that phone call (but nothing to date makes that
evident).

The questions we pose to you are: Is Barack Obama truly an
innovator? Or is he guilty of using warmed over, commoditized
versions of the same old political tactics used for decades by liberal
politicians? Do his innovations really make sense? Or are they ide-
alized versions of creative but impractical ideas? Does Obama lead
by presenting new and bold solutions to America's huge problems?
Or does he dodge them? (e.g., Entitlement costs of Medicare/

Medicaid and Social Security and looming, endless trillion dollar annual deficits.) Does Obama better understand the importance of the right focus yet—and what that focus needs to be? Finally, does President Obama realize that these seemingly old problems are now quite different than similar ones encountered in the past, and his dated FDR-era solutions and Keynesian economics actually makes them worse, and not better?

I think you see the answers to all these questions are still "apparently not." Clearly, innovative leadership is not a talent easily taught or transferred. Lacking the experience and perspective to find new solutions leads to reliance on old, formulaic, but failed solutions. The new problems the USA faces today may resemble the old ones in many respects, but they are not the same—nor are the circumstances that surround them. Thus the new problems demand new solutions—approaches that are quite different from the "warmed over" old ones tried to this point.

The facts say Barack Obama doesn't "get" this difference. One just has to read an account of the Great Depression and how FDR handled the problems—how the solutions used at the time helped to prolong the depression—then compare that to what Obama is doing today. You will be amazed at the similarities. Applying old solutions to new problems is quite a lot like the definition of insanity, and it is just as surely a path to frustration and failure.

As a leader, you must always be innovating, looking for new solutions and ways to stay ahead of competitors, watching the subtle changes in your markets and recognizing the need to constantly change to deal with both of these. You cannot become complacent, because when you do, you will lose. Complacency is the antithesis of leadership. Years ago, when John was President of Huffy Bicycles, they had a saying that seems relevant here, "If you are coasting, you must be going downhill!" You should always be asking, "Is there a new and better, more effective way to solve this new problem?" Remember the three steps to problem solving? A flawed understanding of the problem leads to failed solutions.

A clear understanding seeks improvements on proven effective ways that solved past problems, which we know about and/

or have already used but can adapt and improve to fit the new circumstances we face? (e.g., The Reagan era solutions, but updated to 21st century situations.) Great leaders are problem solvers and thus by nature are innovators. Take the time think through ways you can innovate in your role today. How you can solve problems in better ways? Then think through how you can keep doing that over and over as circumstances and conditions continue to change. (e.g., Starbucks).

And whatever you do, once you have tried something and found it to fail, perhaps more than once, don't keep using that old solution. Adjust and adapt, then evolve. Otherwise, you will truly be guilty of the definition of insanity. Simply observing President Barack Obama's frustration at his failures is evidence enough how he feels—but he knows little else to do about it except make excuses and blame others. What a shame.

OBAMA PRESIDENCY BACKGROUND AND TYPICAL ISSUES

QE1 didn't make much difference in the economy. Perhaps it helped avert a total meltdown—but opinions vary on that. QE2 was smaller and only made a minor difference—temporarily—if that. Stimulus 1 didn't make very much difference either. It was poorly conceived and even more poorly executed. So now the "Jobs Program" proposed by President Obama looks a lot like a smaller, thinly disguised version of Stimulus 2—"lite." It too would make little difference—mostly because it will never get past Congress. Already the Democratically controlled Senate has rejected parts of it. They say, "you learn from experience." The answer to that is, "not necessarily." Only if you reflect on what that experience proved—and disproved—can you learn from it. Otherwise you, too, might become guilty of "the definition of insanity."

෴

"Talk is cheap...except when Congress does It."

—Anonymous

CHAPTER THIRTY-ONE

MAKE THREE ENVELOPES

There is a widely known story in business; some would call it a "joke," but to many, it is not very funny:

> Upon taking a new job, a man is given three numbered envelopes by his predecessor and told: "Open these in number order when you get into trouble." When the first trouble comes, the man opens the envelope number one. In it is a small piece of paper that says, *"Blame your predecessor."* He does that, and it seems to work; his trouble is averted. Then, a few months later, some new trouble crops up. The man opens envelope number two, and the slip of paper shows the advice, *"Blame your staff."* He does so, and that also seems to help remedy the trouble—at least transferring the blame for it from him to others. Finally, after a bit more time has elapsed, bigger trouble comes, and the man reaches frantically for the third envelope and opens it. The note inside says, *"You are toast; you are gone. But before you go, make three numbered envelopes to give your successor."*

The moral of this story is that blaming others seldom works—at least not for very long. It is an attractive trap that always backfires in the end. At this point, Barack Obama has opened his second envelope, and the third is looming not too far off, if he continues leading as he is now. The lesson of the "three envelopes" is "Leadership 101." It simply means that, if you are not ready to take on a position, the good and bad that comes with, and not ready to take full responsibility for the outcomes, don't take it on.

Stopping to think about whether you are ready for the responsibility that comes with a role is something that is too seldom done. A semi-humorous definition of "confidence comes to mind: "The feeling you have just before you realize what you signed up to do." That must be how President Obama secretly feels right now. He fell in love with the idea of the "role" of being president, of the adulation, of being in such an important position, and of having all that power. Who wouldn't? He didn't actually think through whether the role was truly the best fit for him, at that time, given his limited experience. We believe that look of realization came into his eyes briefly, on the stage in front of thousands of cheering supporters. It looked like he was thinking, "Oh my, what have I gotten myself into?"

Obama's only option now is to try his hardest for reelection, to buy himself more time to "finish the job," which in his case would require doing different things than those that have failed thus far. But he only has "one envelope left!" And it's far from clear that he would do many things differently. Barack Obama is already caught on the horns of dilemmas that he cannot cope with. Approving the Keystone Pipeline is clearly a good decision for the USA, and for his union constituents who would get many of the new jobs. But it flies in the face of his environmental supporters. Thus he must make some decision—and not knowing which one to make—he makes one that is essentially a form of procrastination. He stalls in hopes of helping his reelection efforts, and yet he still makes the wrong decision for most Americans.

You would also find it understandably hard to not reach for an immense opportunity like this, if one was offered. The reason is that you may think that if you do not reach for it, and/or accept the role now, you may not get another chance. In many situations that is absolutely right—but that is not a valid reason to take a job, a role or a position that you are not ready for and/or are incapable of performing successfully.

In reality, a lot depends on how you answer, when given the big opportunity. If you just say "No thanks," that might be the end of it. But if you take the time to really think through the magnitude and requirements of the new role, you might be able to show the person offering the position why this is just might not the right time and answer, "No, thank you, not right now. The timing is wrong for me, but one of these days I'll be ready." Then you should seek help in getting ready—for the next time around. You will find that you might get another shot at the position, and be far better prepared for it when you do. Take a position you are not ready for, and you take a great risk. You are very likely to be "making three envelopes!"

For Barack Obama, this was a once-in-a-lifetime shot at the biggest job on the planet. He couldn't say no, even if he knew deep down that he might not be ready for it. It was now or never for Obama. No one knows what he really thought after his victory celebration—except perhaps his wife Michelle, (whose ambitions... and qualifications... may exceed his). During the long and arduous campaign, Obama seemed to grow into his newfound role (but only on the campaign trail), as he convinced himself that he was ready, and then defeated the vaunted Clinton machine and its flag bearer, Hillary Clinton. He even withstood the shots taken by former president Bill Clinton. Of course he had to take the job when he could get it, whether he was ready and fully qualified or not. We are now seeing the consequences of that decision.

NOTE: Defining the qualifications for being president of the USA is something few have even attempted, so knowing what they were was even hard to say—and being able to make stirring speeches was a prominent one—especially during the campaign and election. Obama backers still feel he has done a creditable job as president, in a difficult situation. Unfortunately, all of the real-world metrics say otherwise. Obama himself predicted that if he could not remedy America's ills in 3+ years, he should be looking at a one-term presidency.

Fortunately, things are not quite like this in the business world. Big chances come along, but there is usually more than one chance to "grab for the brass ring." Sometimes, it's better to bide your time and wait for the right opportunity—and one that you are prepared to handle and succeed.

One last piece of very important advice: be conscious of the fact that human nature draws us to want to "be in charge" and have more "power." While this is completely normal, seeking power (alone) can destroy a person. As the saying goes, "Power corrupts, but absolute power, corrupts absolutely." Always be on guard to make sure you have the right motives for why you want something, and why you are doing what you are doing—and that you are not just seeking "more power."

If you deserve to have "more power" it will be because you earned it by your actions, your competence, your courage and your character. No one can bestow power that lasts for long unless it is deserved. Do the right things, for the right reasons, and in the right ways. You will be surprised how much power finds its way to you.

OBAMA PRESIDENCY BACKGROUND AND TYPICAL ISSUES

This story will not have its ending until the 2012 election is over. It is clear now to many people that Barack Obama doesn't truly deserve the power that was bestowed upon him by the electorate. Has he learned the lessons from his mistakes? It doesn't seem he has. Perhaps he will read and think about the chapters in this book. Sooner or later, he will be forced to either change or continue to struggle. His moment of truth will come with the November of 2012 election and the campaign leading up to it. Many of those who supported him still "like him," and think he has done a good job as president, even if they see his failures and his flaws more clearly. When November 2012 rolls around Americans will decide if they have asked Barack Obama to "make three envelopes"—or not.

❧

"Hope is not a strategy—never has been, never will be."

❧

CONCLUSION:

The fundamental point of this short book is embedded in its title: Hope is not a strategy at all. Hope is an intransitive verb, which means: to cherish a desire with anticipation, and/or... to desire with expectation of obtainment and/or... to expect with confidence. Each chapter in the book described one or more "lessons" that apply to the world of business—free enterprise and capitalism—and were derived from the mistakes of the current occupant of the White House, Barack Obama and his administration, czars and appointees. Hopefully, many people who read the book will benefit from the lessons—whether they agree with our positions or not. It is impossible to outline a complete plan for the repair and revitalization of the United States of America, so we will only close with a few paragraphs of the most fundamental nature.

First, a truly successful strategy encompasses far more than "intense desire" or "expectation." It includes clear plans and statements of what must be done to achieve a chosen set of goals and objectives, and continues with how to execute those strategies within timetables and budgets that are set and then observed and managed.

Nowhere does the most desirable strategy for the United States of America include a massive growth of government bureaucracy, funded by deficit spending, which drains taxpayers of prosperity, burdens them with taxes, rules and regulations, while squeezing private investment out of the free markets. Neither does it encompass a large-scale redistribution of wealth according to some neo-Marxist scheme. The Reagan theme of "a rising tide lifts all boats" only requires modification to assure that it truly does "lift all boats" including those of the vast middle class in America, and not just the upper echelon of our economy. The only ways to rein in the current deficit problems are to rein in spending and change the course of the country to grow its way back into solvency. Obama simply has no clue how to do this.

Restoring America to prosperity and global respect requires a deep understanding of what made America great—American exceptionalism, personal freedom and a free enterprise system where opportunity, capital and initiative combine to create economic growth. Economic growth leads to the creation of countless jobs, which is the only way to rebuild the economic middle class in America. Economic growth has been stifled by big government—oppressive regulations, high taxes, irresponsible spending and most recently, a generally anti-business climate in Washington, DC—led and exhibited by President of the United States, Barack Obama.

Obama's campaign theme of "Hope and Change" captured the imagination of millions of Americans. Many of them are now disillusioned, by the realization that it was false hope and negative change, which followed Obama's inauguration and the first three years of his presidency.

To restore America's vitality requires reining in of the large and overbearing government, a restraint of spending to live within our means, the reversion to responsible regulations, a restructuring of our tax base to levy reasonable taxes, an expansive energy policy, a serious plan for controlling immigration and dealing with the millions of illegal immigrants already in America, a restructuring of our foreign relations, national security and defense strategies, and fundamentally, a complete revamping of our system of education.

These kinds of changes are only possible with a pro-free enterprise, growth mentality in our nations capital, and in our nation's leadership. Our leaders must lead. Much of the preceding material—the "lessons" as we call them—are derived from failures of leadership and/or competence.

Fortunately, in a Federal Republic, with free elections, these problems can be remedied. It requires choosing new leadership on a large scale, and then holding that leadership responsible—and accountable—for undoing the past decade of mistakes, and digging our way out of a massive debt burden and overgrown government.

These choices will be neither easy nor popular. The path back to prosperity will be difficult and there will be obstacles and uneven progress—but it is a path we must follow if we are to save our country. There will be shared sacrifices required on the part of all Americans. These must be endured with the prospect that they will lead to better times—times of fiscal and moral responsibility—and of growth and prosperity

Our enemies and dissidents will continue to cause problems for us, and these problems can only get worse, until we get our own house in order. We must face them and deal with them. We must also realize that America can no longer afford to be the planet's global policeman, financier and relief agency. The era of America as hegemon is ending.

We must heal and fix, then strengthen our own country first. America must be more pragmatic than ever about which countries are our friends and allies, which are our enemies, and which are "sitting on the fence" waiting to see if they should join us, take advantage of us or attack us.

These are difficult matters to sort out in these turbulent, and troubled global times—but we have no choice but to sort them out—and then act accordingly. Doing all of this properly and with all prudent speed, will result in the rejuvenation of America, the repatriation of work to create American jobs, and the re-employment of millions of disenfranchised Americans, to do the jobs that are going unfilled now and in the future.

As in any perilous and difficult journey, we will need strong, determined leadership by Americans of courage, character and competence. The journey will require discipline, drive and determination. But the prize for success is worth the effort and the penalty for failure is almost unthinkable.

We believe the lessons in HOPE IS NOT A STRATEGY will help in some small way, because it is our future and that our friends, family, children and grandchildren that is at stake. May God bless the efforts of our country's leaders, that they have the will, wisdom and inspiration to succeed, and may God bless the United States of America.

ᕤᓫ

"Be who you are, because whoever matters doesn't mind, and whoever minds, doesn't matter."[1]

ᕤᓫ

---

[1]   Dr. Seuss

THE LESSONS:

I. LEADERSHIP

1. Style is only more important than substance, temporarily, then substance is required or the style is phony and hollow, coming across as "all hat and no cattle."
2. Speeches are not plans, or strategies, they are just verbalization of them—if there is one; and if there isn't, then speeches are meaningless words with no plan or results
3. Don't change your values to fit your audiences, because audiences vary all over the place, and you will come across as "pandering" and in the end, having no values that are your own.
4. You never win pitting groups in an organization against each other, because all of the people's energy is consumed in negativity, infighting, and politics, with far too little of it going toward achieving positive results.
5. Integrity is your most important asset, perhaps the most basic foundation of everything you stand for; with it you can do great things, and without it, you will ultimately be nothing.
6. What do you do when nobody is following your lead? Consider that you may not be a leader deserving of being followed and resolve to learn how to better lead if you can.

II. EXPERIENCE AND PEOPLE

7. There's no substitute for real experience, because nothing else prepares you for the range of challenges you will face and the resourcefulness you will need to use.

8. You are only as good as the people you surround yourself with, because one person alone, can do very little. Everyone must rely on others; if the others are the wrong ones, nothing good happens after that.

9. You are known by the company you keep, and that will brand you with a reputation that you cannot shake; choose your company wisely and well.

10. Stay humble, and don't believe your own hype, because it is seldom something you can deliver on consistently. Hype is, by definition, over-promising on what you can deliver. That is a very bad practice indeed.

11. Beware the pretender because they are never what they seem to be, and usually cannot be trusted in matters of any importance. If they could, they wouldn't need to pretend.

III. TRUTH AND CONSEQUENCES

12. Words and how you use them are powerful, and people often take you at your word until you prove to them that your words cannot be trusted. Those who hear your words read everything you mean into them, and a lot more.

13. Be prepared to deal with the consequences of your actions, to take responsibility for mistakes and failures and to be accountable for the results you committed to delivering. To do anything less would be a failure of ethics and integrity.

14. When you don't have the answer—don't try to sound like you do—because there is no credible way to get out of that kind of fakery. People will then doubt everything you claim to know—whether your answers are true or fabrications.

15. Take responsibility for your actions—and your mistakes— and learn from them. There is no escaping the consequences of mistakes, and the more you try to squirm out

of them, the worse you will look. Own your actions and if wrong, admit it—up front and honestly.

16. There are no successful victims, since victims are, by definition failing due to someone else's actions, or their inaction. Either is a tacit admission of failure, which is inescapable.

IV. MISTAKES AND MISUNDERSTANDINGS

17. Noble intentions don't justify screwing up, because no matter how noble they were, there comes with them the responsibility to deliver on those intentions. Think carefully before announcing grand plans based on noble intentions and no knowledge of how to deliver on them.

18. If something is too big to fail, it will! And the bigger it is, the harder it will fall and the bigger mess it will make. Think big, but try small, and adjust for miscalculations. Then go big—but not too big. Don't "bet everything" on anything.

19. Throwing money at problems doesn't fix them, but is a common and attractive "rookie mistake." Money alone doesn't solve much, unless it is combined with solid strategy, execution, leadership and a clear plan objective.

20. All spending is not "investment"—some of it is just "spending." Many expenses are wasted or unproductive spending. Some investments have little, no or negative returns. Even all "investment spending" is not good spending. It must earn a decent return.

21. Victory by definition isn't victory; it is a delusion or at best an illusion created by trying to change the measurements after the fact. When there is little definition up front, it is easy to claim a different "victory" but invariably, the real world exposes this as a trick.

V. HOPE IS NOT A STRATEGY

22. Change for change sake can be harmful. Worse than that is it can be downright stupid. Change is disruptive, sometimes even destructive, and always difficult and unsettling. Change should be treated as the powerful medicine it can be—and handled with care.

23. Wishing doesn't make it happen, in fact, this too creates either delusion or denial. Wishing can be powerful because it is not constrained by reality—until it must be executed and something done about the wish. Then the trouble starts.

24. Tactical executives lose...strategic executives win—in the long term. Tacticians may appear to make short-term progress. However, in the longer-term this progress may not be progress at all, and may need to be reversed and completely redone. That is the purpose of strategies—deciding what to do first, then using tactics in the execution.

25. The Humpty-Dumpty principle is painfully true. An organization, a company, a country's government or any entity—large or small—once "broken" simply cannot be "put back together again," because time changes everything. What once worked, will not work any more—and neither will the people whose lives and careers were "broken." They will never be the same either.

26. Understand your customer before you try to sell them something. Unless you clearly understand your customers' needs, wants and motivations, you are as likely to try selling them the wrong thing as the right one—with devastating consequences. They become someone else's customer.

VI. TIMELESS TRUTHS

27. Take care of the stakeholders...they'll take care of you. These are the people who have trusted you, followed you and invested in you. If you don't take care of them, they will have no reason to take care of you—and they won't— they'll leave.

28. Lack of focus will sink you, because there are only three resources that must be allocated to accomplish anything: time, talent and treasure (money). No focus means wasting at least some, and maybe many of these on the wrong things, starving the right ones for critically needed resources. Work on the wrong thing, spend on the wrong thing, and take too long on the wrong thing, and there is no recovery.

29. Accountability will make you because people respect someone who is willing to be held accountable—and vice versa. Losers make promises, which they may or may not keep. Winners make commitments for which they are willing to be held accountable.

30. The definition of insanity: doing the same thing over and over and expecting a different outcome," is no joke. It happens time and again. If at first you don't succeed, try, try again—but not exactly the same way—pay attention to why you didn't succeed and adjust.

31. Make three envelopes is a not so funny story about how you get only three strikes, in baseball and in business, and after the third one, you are "out." That means you'd better not try to blame others for your mistakes on strikes one and two, because you are either in denial or incompetent.

32. **Hope is not a strategy. It is a word that expresses a desire and a wish. Without a strategy it is a hollow promise, that will not be kept—and that is the greatest lesson learned from the Obama presidency.**

౷

"Government was created to work for the American people, not vice versa."

౷

Two Authors,
Two Different Generations...
One Message

Dave M. Lukas is a modern day "Renaissance Man." Recently turned 30, he is an accomplished speaker, entrepreneur and investor. He has been published in numerous publications, including Forbes alongside John Mariotti, and is known for his no-nonsense, common sense approach. He has been invited to work with thought leaders such as Brian Tracy, Tony Robbins, Zig Ziglar, and many others. He also frequently speaks on the mindset of success and the everyday principles of strategic leadership and business growth.

He founded his first business at a very young age (5 years old!) and continued to develop successful businesses through college. Dave then took that early success to a national F500 company where he earned recognition as Rookie of the Year, Sales Consultant of the Year, Top 25 Producer (out of 1500 sales reps). Today, Dave consults with companies at all stages of growth, often taking ownership positions, which allows him to have maximum personal impact on strategic growth targets. As Vice President and co-owner of Grasp Technologies, for example, Dave has architected 100% growth every year for each of the last 5 years. Dave feels most at home when helping people learn new skills, or reach new levels of personal accomplishment. He holds a BA in Management and Finance from Baldwin Wallace College.

John L. Mariotti is an Internationally recognized executive, author and speaker. During his 48-year career, he led major businesses as President of Huffy Bicycles, and later as Group President of Rubbermaid Office Products Group, and later built a successful consulting practice. He was also Chairman of World Kitchen, Inc., on whose board he still serves. John has served on multiple corporate boards and consulted with and advised many well-known American companies.

He has written hundreds of articles, spoken to thousands, and authored 9 business books including The Power of Partnerships, Smart Marketing, and two award winners: The Shape-Shifters and The Complexity Crisis, which was chosen one of 2008's Best Books for Small Business. He writes weekly blogs for American Express—Open Forum, for Forbes—Prosper Now, and his own THE ENTERPRISE—Telling It Like It is. His latest book, a novel on cyber-terrorism is The Chinese Conspiracy, released in Jan. 2011. John holds a B. S. M. E., from Bradley University and an M. S. M. E. from the University of Wisconsin.

John lives in Central Ohio with his wife of 47 years 3 children and 5 grandchildren. He also enjoys helping businesses and people become more successful. Like Dave, he cares deeply about the USA and its future

www.ingramcontent.com/pod-product-compliance
Lightning Source LLC
Chambersburg PA
CBHW051503170526
45166CB00001B/372